THE LIMITS OF SOCIALISM

BY

O. FRED BOUCKE

Professor of Economics at Pennsylvania State College

New York

THE MACMILLAN COMPANY

1920

Set up and electrotyped. Published April, 1920.

PREFACE

At the present time the general reader will, the author believes, be interested in some of the following questions which socialism has sought to answer in its own peculiar way. First, to what extent can the income of the average man be raised under socialism, as contrasted with the present individualistic régime? Second, if any marked change in national income is to be expected from socialism, in what direction will it most naturally occur, and what are the limits set to this endeavor? Third, is it true that socialism can establish a democracy in the political sense such as individualism has not as yet pretended to have realized? Fourth, is Marxian economics an indispensable basis to the program mapped out by socialists, or is the refutation of such doctrine, as hitherto submitted by professional economists, a relatively unimportant step which in no wise invalidates the general outlook of socialists? Fifth, if socialism is a theory of prosperity, what is the scientific basis for it, and, more particularly, what data has present day science to offer in support of the thesis expressed or implied by socialism, that a rational method for socio-economic reform exists? Sixth, what are the ultimate questions which socialism has attempted to answer, or must feel obliged to discuss hereafter, in order to find a logical groundwork for its demands?

These and some other outstanding topics have been given consideration in the following pages, and it is hoped that in them will be found a review, from partly new standpoints, of what is most important in socialistic platforms. The fourth and fifth chapters contain foundations for all later ones. On them the treatment of the whole subject largely rests. However, it is hoped that the summary which opens the last chapter will furnish a convenient guide to some of the main points advanced, and in this way make clearer the idea of limits in socialism, within which socialists hand in hand with social scientists may continue their studies, but beyond which progress is less certain and more open to the sort of criticism which up to date has injured the socialist cause.

State College, Pa.

TABLE OF CONTENTS

PART I
THE LIMITS IN THEORY

PART II
THE LIMITS IN PRACTICE

CONTENTS

LIST OF TABLES

THE LIMITS OF SOCIALISM

CHAPTER I

THE PROBLEM

§ 1. **General Statement of the Problem.**— Social science has to do with social processes. It studies the facts of social life and seeks to discover whatever principles of general validity and permanent operation may underlie them. The sociologist and economist notably are interested in this side of the subject. Each studies the phenomena and looks for laws with a possible view to application. The basic sciences for them are biology and psychology. After they have laid down the fundamentals obtaining in social life the statesman may try to make use of them for his own purposes. Politics is then the science dealing with the application of principles formulated by sociology and economics.

This is one way of stating the sociological problem in general. A second is the common sense view which simply asks: Are there any social evils? Is there anything to correct in the life of individuals or nations? If so, how may it be done? As regards the evils, are they inherent in life or are they eradicable? Are they of personal making or should we look for their explanation in certain objective conditions over which the individual has no control? In so far as evils are removable, shall we rely upon one major remedy relative to which all others are merely auxiliary, or is the cure to be effected by calling to aid many forces for betterment, no one of them sufficient by itself, but their joint effect being a regeneration of society?

At all times we have these questions to face, because evils always have existed and likely always will exist. If the word evil is rightly understood, its complete elimination will not be expected by any scientist. There is always room for improvement; we shall never adjust ourselves to our surroundings perfectly.

§ 2. **The Socialistic Platform in the United States.**—Socialism is a doctrine and a movement for reform which has seen some of the deeper aspects of the problem and tried to solve them in a rather unique way, by abolishing capitalism. The core of socialism is the abolition of private property in production and distribution, and the substitution for it of public ownership. The public in general, and not particular individuals, are to own the means by which goods are produced and exchanged. This subversion of one régime, and the introduction of another in which the capitalist is superseded by the state or by the community, is the central theme of socialists.

Socialism however is more than one single thing. It is not simply a theory, but also a movement for redress of evils. It is preaching and practice in one. It is the enumeration of evils, their explanation, and a prescription for betterment. Socialism consists of an indictment, a theory, and a platform for propaganda and eventual realization. Socialists have a creed which guides their conduct, and in this respect they are much stronger than many other would-be reformers. Scientific socialism is scientific because it properly inquired into the Why of affairs before proposing to get at the How.

The socialistic attitude may be illustrated from a simile in a charming book written by Edward Bellamy.[1]

[1] Bellamy, E., "Looking Backward," p. 10.

Society there is compared to a coach driven by Hunger and dragged on a seemingly interminable highway by a throng of toilers. What a hilly road it is! What windings and obstacles ahead. What a wearisome journey for the common folk!

On top of the coach ride a few privileged ones who enjoy themselves to their hearts' content. They admire the beauty of the landscape on each side of the road, and fill their lungs with exhilarating breezes. They do not gaze too fondly upon the embarrassment of the team below, for the spectacle of distress jars on their delicate sensibilities. They are willing of course to dress the wounds of those bruised by the ceaseless straining in harness, but they wish to keep the vehicle moving at all costs, and they spur on the laggards with false words of cheer.

Yet they do not always remain in their seats, nor are all those below condemned to perpetual toil. An exchange of seats does take place from time to time. Some of the throng, perhaps, manage to slough off the shackles which bind them, and succeed in climbing to the top. They then join the crowd of joyriders and are received with more or less coolness. Or some of the privileged ones suddenly come to the end of their life's journey and bequeath their rights to those below waiting anxiously for the favor.

A seat on top is what everybody wants. And yet no one there is really happy, for all are trembling in everlasting fear of a disaster. At every turn of the road, at every blocking of the track, they shake with trepidation lest the coach be upset and a painful ending meet them below. They enjoy their advantages such as an unequal assignment of labors may give, but they face the future pessimistically, because their conscience smites them.

Socialists have accepted the picture as substantially

socialists

true to life. They have called attention to the inequalities in social arrangements and demanded a change for the better. They have insisted upon an upsetting of the coach because they see no other way out of the difficulty. The socialistic theory of progress has been formulated to make this clear.

Scientific socialism comprises four points of theory that formerly were considered essentials for its success as a political party in action. It was the first of sociological doctrines to preach that prosperity must be measured by wealth, that all social relations turn on facts of wealth and its production or exchange, that evils are the result of a maladjustment socially grounded, and that a revolution was impending because of a universal law which no man and no act of legislation could defy. This is in large part the significance of socialism. It taught us to connect our moral ratings with the economic facts of life. It pointed out the paramount importance of income for purposes of self realization. It treated the problem of misery objectively, and yet humanized it by holding man responsible rather than nature. And finally it exemplified the might of maladjustment by showing how private property under different systems of production could have entirely different results for the masses of the people. From this many things followed, but one of them notably was the value of sociological analysis and the need of enlightenment which should remedy evils before a law of evolution did so abruptly.

Marxian economics and Marx's interpretation of history have been mainly associated with socialism. It has been held that the economics expounded by Marx in his Capital was the making or marring of socialism, and that socialism loses its usefulness, becomes a failure, if certain contentions in the theory of value or in the economic interpretation of the past could be proven untenable. In this spirit mere details have often been magnified into decisive issues, or what were salient features have been made the test by which to settle once and for all the questions of social reform. Yet it is significant, and it should be well noted by the critics of early — let us say dogmatic — socialism, that the arguments of Karl Marx have been in large part abandoned by his successors without weakening in the least their ardor, or the chance of their achieving unusual things. This alone should have disillusioned those who thought that the end of the Marxian system meant the death-knell of the socialistic movement. It manifestly could not mean that.

Since 1890 the German socialists have said little about surplus value and much about political rights. Opportunism has diluted scientific socialism, but it has given a new lease of life to the main assertion of socialists that great evils exist, that they are widespread and perceived by the masses; and that the socialization of capital will alone relieve mankind of its social diseases.

The war has further modernized socialistic demands, besides putting practice in the foreground; and in the United States it has widened the vision of reformers, so that to-day American socialism is stronger theoretically and practically than ever.

The party platform of 1918 [2] calls for the federation of all nations with a view to ending wars. It pleads for a uniform monetary system for all the world, for the devising of machinery to adjust credit to international needs, for the reduction of armaments, and for an international minimum wage scale. Those things in particular are to be made the concern of all nations in an endeavor to promote universal goodwill and peace.

2 Congressional Platform of the (American) Socialist Party, 1918.

In addition however many other demands are made, some of them familiar and approved by the founders of socialism, and others of recent origin, the result of conditions which Marx could not foresee. We have again, for instance, the clarion call for a nationalization of private capital, without which socialists would lose their most distinctive mission. Public utilities and basic industries including mines, grain elevators, stockyards, and banks are specifically enumerated as preferential subjects for socialization.

Other items of note are the abolition of child labor, a reduction of the working day commensurate with technical progress, the official recognition of a national minimum wage, the extension of the right to strike and to boycott, the appointment of shop committees with representation of labor, the introduction of free vocational education, gratuitous insurance of all workers, both rural and urban, against accident and sickness, and the guarantee of employment to all who seek it.

These are the main economic rights which socialism to-day grants to the working classes, and the acknowledgment of which by the state is the goal socialists are aiming at. They come first and overshadow certain political reforms that are also urged, but which, we may be sure, will follow automatically once the economic rights of the citizen are put into operation.

§ 3. **Leading Questions for Socialism.**—The question is: Are these demands fair? Do they harmonize with socialistic theory? Or more to the point, are they agreeable to the data of social science which socialism has always made it a point to consult in the framing of political and economic platforms?

One may, to begin with, put this more concretely by asking what socialism promises in case it is given a free hand, and how much of its promise is realizable. *Granting the socialization of capital*, what can socialism do to root out evil and improve our living? According to its own admission the facts of production, exchange and control occupy a preëminent place in any scheme of meliorism. If then the socialist is confident of accomplishing by his system what heretofore we have not managed to do, on what grounds does he make his promises?

As to production, e. g., can socialism produce so much more than individualism? And in what kinds of goods is the gain to come? As to distribution, what is meant by a new principle in the pricing of goods and services? In how far may socialism ensure each man his product, when the competitive régime fails to do so? What are the limits in measurement of values and services? What is to define for us a need, according to which family budgets will be made out?

Or take the problem of consumption and of control. What will socialism mean by consumption that the orthodox economist has not meant by it? *To what extent can economic income regulate psychic outgo?* How far may we hope for race improvement by means of socialistic reforms? And in what sense can socialism make democracy real, when up to date it has been a mere sham, or at best a modest approximation to a lofty ideal? Can the people be led to direct themselves politically? Is the prospect of perpetual peace bright enough, so that our time hallowed traditions of nationalism may give way to a more generous view of mankind?

Such are immediate practical questions that the socialistic theory inspires. But, in the second place, it prompts us to meet squarely the far broader problem whether a *rationale of meliorism* really *exists?* Is it possible, and why and within what limits, to establish principles of reform which shall satisfy our craving for justice and social welfare at a given moment? Is reform, in other words, a matter of science, or of whim and hazard without possibility of guidance? Do we feel wrongs without having redress elsewhere than in our personal adjustments, or is there a way for governing people so that the welfare of the largest number becomes feasible and normal?

This larger phase of the socialistic movement forces us to search into the nature of knowledge, into the relation of social aspects which the founders of socialism so bluntly stated and sought to demonstrate to a critical world. It is ultimately a matter of psychology and sociology, if by the latter term we may designate the sum total of investigations into social man. However, the psychological data may be divided into the logical and the psychological or biological, and the first then asks: What is our knowledge, how do we reason, and what is the meaning of laws and causation? And the second then treats of the subjective interpretation of the social process. Man of necessity is in the center of things. The social student invariably will go wrong unless he considers all sociological and economic data an expression of living men and women, whose innermost nature is the key to any problem that may present itself.

An answer to socialism hence involves an inquiry into the process of learning by which stimuli become response and thoughts are converted into actions of enduring value. It is for the critic of, or sympathizer with, socialistic teachings to picture the relation between economic and non-economic conditions as an individual experience. Only in this manner can the Marxian interpretation be rectified in the modern scientific spirit. Only by this route shall we succeed in tracing the real connection between historical events which to some seem not at all related, and to others are almost identical. If socialists dwelled on the causative force of methods of production, were they wrong or right? Was the relation stated correctly, or is civilization an organic whole whose parts the historian may not separate on any excuse?

The wider treatment of the question of meliorism leads to a conception of progress and prosperity not altogether opposed to the notions held by early socialists. It must be part of the would-be reformer's education to define prosperity, since Marxian philosophy is so incisive on that point. It is necessary to appreciate its view of misery as an integral part of an outlook developed *not by economics, but by metaphysics*. It is inevitable indeed that a contemplation of socialistic ideals and promises suggests an answer to the query: What is the ultimate good, what is justice, and what is the bearing of science on norms of life that under individualism as well as under socialism are reflected in acts of the legislature?

Socialism, since it is a theory of prosperity, implies all these questions, and more. It compels us to take a long view of things, not a near at hand view individualistically trumped up. Socialism is stern and bold. It boasts a noble intellectual lineage, and will not be put off or downed by flippant banter. Complacency cannot undo the ills that are known to exist, and an appeal to national traditions will deceive none except the thoughtless ones. Socialism is neither a chimera nor a crime, though by a few it has been considered both.

The need for reform seems universally conceded. But whether it is or not, the reality of the larger problem no one can deny. It *is* worth while to know whether social evils have causes that we can specifically unearth and offset by remedial measures. It is important to decide whether politics is more than a game among fighting cocks. It does pique the curiosity of many good folk to see illegalities and absurd criminality flourishing in this age of enlightenment. They involuntarily ask: Is it unavoidable, or may we right things by using our wits?

The world to-day is in ferment. The war has set people's teeth on edge, and the post-war effects are not calculated to soothe their feelings on sundry matters. The terrible, the unbelievable, the overwhelming fact remains that many millions had to die innocently in a stupendous struggle that the achievements of the nineteenth century should have made impossible. Whatever we may think of the war just concluded, of its causes and instigators, of its political consequences or costs in material and men, the one great question is now before us. We must know whether the social process logically involves such disasters, or whether the safety and welfare of the masses may be procured by rational means at the disposal of government, supposing social science continues its labors.

Socialism has many times replied to our questions. It has placed the blame on a certain form of economic organization and pledged itself to deliver us from all evil if we please to listen to its sermon. Social scientists can do no better than to think of socialists as students who desire to substitute sense for sentiment in reforming man. Whether they have struck the right path, whether socialism alone will do, whether science can espouse a collectivistic program favoring some of the demands voiced by socialists, these are questions that at the present moment confront us. The ultimate place of science in social reform cannot be determined just now, but its bearing on socialism is self evident.

CHAPTER II

KARL MARX AND THE ECONOMISTS

§ 1. **Marx as an Eclectic.**— Marx's Kapital is considered an offshoot of English classic economics, whose chief exponents are Smith, Ricardo, Senior, and J. S. Mill. The connection between especially Ricardo and Marx is so obvious that it seems hardly necessary to trace out other lines of descent. Yet it is by no means true that the individualistic scheme of economics as it prevailed at the beginning of the nineteenth century was logically essential to Kapital. Rather, if one excepts the labor doctrine of value, there is scarcely any point of prime importance in Ricardo's Principles that reappears in the German work. The Bible of socialism uses English economics mainly to refute or recast it, not to build with it a theory for fighting capitalism. That was surely quite out of the question.

One may explain this difference in another way by noting Marx's essentials of character, for plainly he was an iconoclast by inborn temperament who saw everywhere idols and images where others lingered reverently, and whose one mission seemed to be to dethrone the false gods. Marx seldom was satisfied with what he saw about him. He was an idealist in spite of his crass materialistic system of sociological thought. To him it was painful to see people practice quite the opposite of what they preached, to hear them expound theories that nowhere squared with the facts, while attempting to hide their real sentiments under a mask of scholarly impartiality. He sought to go beneath the surface of things and see what was really at stake, but in so doing he usually encountered truths that rankled because those most obligated to honor them proved their worst enemies.

Marx was a man of great acumen and incredible capacity for work. He could read hundreds of books within a short time and digest most of what was significant in them. He would listen to many men but ultimately go his own way. He borrowed without plagiarizing, and he returned with interest the principal which he openly made use of. Whatever passed through the alembic of his mind came out as a product distinctly his own. He took pieces here and there, but never all. Thus from Hegel he took the dialectic, but inverted his order of syllogisms. He rejoiced in Bentham's positivism, but scoffed at his individualistic norm of utilitarianism. Of Proudhon he had, with respect to some of his preachings, a high opinion, but see how he ranted at What Is Property! Feuerbach gave him inspiration and definite ideas as to the meaning of the dialectic process, but for all that he turned away from the Essence of Christianity. The naturalistic philosophy excited his admiration in so far as it combated transcendentalism, but beyond that he had as little use for it as Hume or Blackstone. In all instances he listened attentively at first, but before long found flaws that invalidated most of what to others seemed valuable.

Thus it was that in spite of the remarkable stage of perfection which the economic science had reached in Marx's days, little of it is constructively incorporated in the Critique of 1859. The physiocrats had written their ponderous tomes, Smith and Ricardo had established firmly the principles of competitive economics, the reaction against Manchestrianism had yielded some notable results both among the French and the English, and in Germany the Historical School was beginning to develop a philosophy of methods. Yet none of it furnishes foundations for Karl Marx. Instead he takes a bit here and a bit there. He nibbles and absorbs a detail, or plows diligently over a vast field and then claims no fruits whatsoever.

The naturalistic view he could not entertain seriously because it meant statics, and he saw in the social process everywhere motion and conflict. The utilitarian norms were repugnant to him because they smacked of sentimentalism, or of professions of faith that had nothing to do with stern reality. His one hobby was the majesty of logic. The logic of events overawed him, if anything ever did. He saw regularity and necessity where others looked for willed plans subjectively valuated. He had no patience with the slogan which would change the world by giving it an emotional gruelling. People, he argued, should not thus be fed and broken in.

As for the movement fostered by Hildebrandt and Knies, he considered it a children's play because it worked with nationalistic premises, its chief aim being the economic development of Germany. Marx detested such an outlook. The world to him seemed too large to be bounded by race prejudices, and on the other hand he could not approve of a school which catered more to nationalism at any cost than to internationalism on behalf of helpless masses. So, while taking some note of Roscher and his colleagues, he bantered with them lightly, content to pass their notions over with a sarcastic remark at opportune moments, while immersing himself deeply in the radical literature of Thompson, Hodgskin, Bray, and Gray. What these men had penned in their admiration for the French revolutionary spirit he thought over carefully, with consequences known to students of socialism. But even their suggestions did not enslave him. He was impressed, it appears, with their collectivistic treatment of a problem which the disciples of Ricardo so despised, but he went decidedly farther, besides bringing in thoughts no mere economist would have tried to master.

And so, in a most serious sense, also with his use of Ricardian tenets. He read and digested thoroughly what this banker had said, but in the end he disagreed with him on most important points. Much he openly rejected and criticized as utter nonsense. The rest he put to such novel uses that Ricardo would probably not have recognized his contributions in "Das Kapital." Living amidst substantially like environments their teachings yet go far apart. What Marx saw in his long stay in London did not give him the convictions voiced so modestly in Ricardo's Principles. There were similarities between the two that might have augured well for a correspondence of views, but there existed differences, no less, that in the end made them strangers. Their premises were not altogether the same, and for this reason they emphasized different facts in the world about them.

To follow this thought of likeness and unlikeness a little farther — for it is rather interesting — Ricardo might very well be called an optimist, complacently active, who thought the world the best possible, considering the laws of nature, and looked after his business on Exchange. Marx was a pessimist who could see nothing good in the world that treated the laboring classes so shabbily. But on the other hand he looked forward to a change brought about by a law of evolution of universal validity, while Ricardo for all his serene temperament was the stout defender of a law of diminishing returns which condemned the masses forever to a hand-to-mouth living. This was certainly a gloomy outlook. No wonder men spoke of the "dismal science" of economics.

Both Ricardo and Marx were Jews converted to Christianity, but neither professed to have understood all of the adopted creed. Both were men of outstanding personality and mind, men who could think in abstract terms and pack a wealth of heterogeneous facts into a few concepts. Because they towered so far above the general run of people they had little confidence in its rantings and judgments. They did not think the average man capable of sustained mental labors. They despised the sentimentalities of the mob, however sympathetic they were toward their hardships which they witnessed with sorrow and tried sincerely to ease. Both were generous and modest, unostentatious and averse to publicity. Both disliked false show, and especially pseudo sentiments which they sometimes detected where no one else could. Marx derided the moralism of the Benthamites, but in his own home he was the most exemplary of husbands and fathers, punctilious to a fault, and as conventional in matters of morality as he was a free lance in theorizing. Like Ricardo he was a formalist, a stickler for niceties in reasoning, but the most convivial of friends. Like Ricardo he was a leader among men, a leader in thought, a prophet who foresaw the future. Like Ricardo he worked indefatigably on behalf of truth; only while Ricardo supported the government Marx labored to subvert it. Marx was only a few years old when Ricardo died. Had they been contemporaries acquainted with each other's work, it would seem that they should have gotten along very well together, even if they parted company as philosophers.

§ 2. **Ricardian Economics.**— Ricardo in his "Principles of Political Economy" modified at important points the Smithian tradition. He called attention to many inconsistencies in his predecessor's statement, but he agreed with him in one all important respect, namely he accepted the institution of private property as an indispensable part of his economic environment. Adam Smith had not questioned this either. He had thought it sufficiently justified by the facts of human nature which he studied at leisure long before he wrote his Inquiry. In stating his Theory of the Moral Sentiments he had dwelt long on the innate goodness of man. He was greatly impressed with the reality of an altruistic instinct in men, which prompted them to do right — even if at times they fell from grace. To Smith the selfish and the social sentiments were pretty well balanced. There was no fear that society would go to ruin as long as each was left to his own devices as producer and consumer. Discretion, he thought, would win the day. But as against the slight risks of self-assertion he placed the menace of tyrannical government. Only if men are permitted to enjoy the fruit of their labor will they strive to please others and to progress. However unfortunate the disappearance of communism — and he hints now and then at the burdens of entail and primogeniture — private capitalism had its virtues. It was folly to study wealth relations on any other basis.

Ricardo was satisfied with this view, and so it was natural that his definitions of value and capital should be the competitive concepts which economists have learned to respect. The determination of price is left to supply and demand, but the value of a good in the long run is the amount of labor involved in its production. Labor costs measure exchange value. This is the rule. The exceptions are monopoly, as for instance in the ownership of non-reproducible articles — artworks, old vintage, etc.— and the effect of durable machinery which would vary according to its nature and use. Capital as well as land are genuine producers. They are agents essential to the creation of values like labor itself. Consequently these factors are entitled to a share in the national output. Whatever the income is, that must be divided among the several agents so that production may continue. From the competitive standpoint, furthermore, productivity is a rate of production per unit of cost in labor and material spent, though the materials embody past labor. It is therefore with values that Ricardo deals mainly, and not with concrete stuffs or with service as such. The aim of the agents is maximum output of *values*, not of physical things.

The physical aspect becomes important in only one respect, namely when the ratio of food supply to the population is considered; but here its importance is so engrossing that virtually the whole distributive scheme is determined by it. For ever since the Malthusian doctrine found acceptance among economists as a law explaining wars and disease it also furnished the clue to the puzzles of distribution. It was now perfectly evident that people had little to eat chiefly because they would marry and rear children. This alone kept them at starvation's door. The sex impulses being so much more dominant than any other appetite men must work harder each generation to procure a minimum food supply, regardless of what benefits might accrue to them from technical improvements in another field. The law of diminishing returns in agriculture, after a certain point of maximum yield relative to the effort had been passed, punished the thoughtless masses and proved a veritable goldmine to the proprietors of the one indispensable means of production, to wit land.

The landlord profited by the stinginess of nature. He pocketed the difference between the return on the worst land under cultivation and the yield of his own superior land. Against the rapacious landlord, therefore, must be pitted the enterpriser and the wage earner: the former because competition tended to reduce his profits to a minimum scarcely better than a decent livelihood, and the latter because in spite of all inventions he could not improve his daily board. He was bound to live frugally, so the owner of the natural resources might live in splendor. The outlook was a discouraging one, but what could be done about it? It seemed, nothing. Our only hope could be a further diversification of products, and perhaps in the very distant future a restraint of the sex-passions, so that the masses might have somewhat more meat and wheat to consume. But of general affluence there could be no question.

Ricardo does not differentiate clearly between the shares going to capital and those of enterprise, but he informs us that both will gradually shrink, while labor, being already at its lowest, will hold its own. To try to improve the wage earner's lot would be folly, for laws of nature militate against such a plan. "Wages, like other contracts, should be left to the fair and free competition of the market, and should never be controlled by the interference of the legislature."[1] Such is the verdict handed down from the court of classic economy.

§ 3. **Marxian Economist.**— But to Marx all this was cant, or else nothing but shameful ignorance. He retorts in a manner the classic economists never approved of. Namely he refuses to lay social evils at the door of the individual laborer, and instead holds the capitalist to be the malfeasant. He begins by denying what Ricardo

[1] Ricardo, D., "Principles of Political Economy," ch. 5.

took for granted, and ends by asserting what to Ricardo would have been incomprehensible. In other words, he starts with the question: What does *private* capitalism lead to that *socialized* capital would *not* permit? And he suggests the answer by opening his monumental work with a discussion of the exchange process which makes prices out of utility, and profit out of labor.

There is some evidence to show that Marx was influenced by the critics of the Ricardian system who wrote in the first third of the nineteenth century. W. Thompson, for instance, published his "Inquiry into the Principles of the Distribution of Wealth" in 1824. Like others on the continent he had learned from the French Revolution and continued the work carried on by the naturalists who harped on the rights of man. But in England liberalism naturally took an economic turn. Thompson thus followed the mechanistic concepts of the French encyclopedists chiefly for the purpose of illustrating the nobility of labor. A common element was to be found in all kinds of occupation, no matter how intellectual it might be in fact or in appearance. He writes: "What is thought but motion produced and felt in the brain?"[2] and thereby challenges the opinion that different sorts of work are incomparable. To Thompson and to Hodgskin, his colleague, labor is at bottom only one thing. It is expenditure of energy and therefore measurable for purposes of distribution.

It is not unlikely that Marx obtained some of his ideas from this group of writers. But, if so, it is certain that

[2] Thompson, W., "Inquiry into the Principles of the Distribution of Wealth, Preliminary Observations," 1824. See also Bray, J., "Labor's Wrongs and Labor's Remedies, 1839," from which Marx quotes at length in his "Misery of Philosophy," written in 1846. A large part of the Marxian viewpoint is also to be found in Gray, J., "The Social System, 1831."

he went much farther in his use of the physical notion of labor, for he deliberately lumps all classes of labor and arrives at a unit of "socially necessary labor" by summation and division. He tells us in the first pages of his book that "skilled labor counts only as simple labor *intensified*." [3] That is to say, instead of two measures of a product the skilled laborer turns out three or four in the same time; but otherwise his contribution is on a par with that of the jack-of-all-trades. He furthermore defines for us the term "socially necessary" labor. He urges that it comprises three elements always, viz., strictly *human* effort, *valuable* effort, and outlay of *energy*.[4] All labor, he insists, is of man. Labor is the source of all wealth. Nothing is produced, but the hand or mind of man has exerted energy which roughly is measurable and may be imputed to joint producers. But he granted that unless turned to productive uses an expenditure of physical force (Arbeitskraft) would not yield values.

Production being thus made possible by labor solely it followed that machinery was not a productive agent, and hence that capitalists had no just claim to the social dividend. Capital, Marx argued, was but solidified labor. It was labor in concrete form; labor that had crystallized as salts might crystallize from a solution. Capital was mere congealed labor, and hence the owner of capital had no right to its products.

Marx devoted endless pages to showing that capital was but a by-product of competition and of the contract system of production which the champions of Laissez Faire had popularized by their ingenious treatises. To him capital was nothing if not the fruit of laws whose very ex-

[3] Marx, K., "Capital," as published by Ch. Kerr & Co., vol. 1, p. 51.

[4] *Ibidem*, ch. 1, passim.

istence should be justified first, but which the facts of production could not justify. "Capital," he exclaimed, "is dead labor that vampire-like fattens on the blood of living labor." Capital was no more than legalized robbery. It was a wolf in sheepskin, a license to steal, an interloper in honest business, a letter patent for mulcting the real producer of his wealth, and a system of pillage whose ramifications threatened to undermine the social order. What Ricardo had attributed to the blind workings of a merciless law of nature Marx connected exclusively with a faulty economic régime, albeit one which could be overthrown and replaced by a more logical one, if the masses would but pause to think.

In "Capital" the anomalous position of private property is pictured less forcefully than in earlier essays, but it is still emphasized that private property was once in its place, and has lost its rights only because the methods and means of production were changed in principle during the century immediately preceding the Marxian analysis. Between 1750 and 1850, it is pointed out, the self-sufficiency of the laborer has given way to a minute division of labor, so that trade is everything and the handicraft of the individual little or nothing. While one man could turn out a finished article, or as long as the joint authors of a product jointly owned the tools they worked with, private ownership was natural and harmless. But it ceased to be innocuous when mechanical power and intricate machinery did away with the need of muscle and simple tools.[5] To put the ownership of the means of production now in the hands of a few men meant to enslave the worker who had nothing to offer but labor-power.

[5] See, e.g., *ibidem,* vol. I, pp. 88–91, and wellknown passage in "Holy Family."

Henceforth exploitation began and enriched the non-worker under the protection of contract and law.

Theoretically Marx had only contempt for the Malthusian formula. He could not tolerate its implications for fear of losing the main plank in his economic platform. Yet it appears ever and anon that the subsistence wage of the proletariat had no other solid foundation than its preference for a large family, or at least for sex indulgence, to a table freighted with good things to eat. It should, then, be understood that Ricardo after all led Marx into his central position, even though from a desire for consistency this was loudly denied. Marx in fact consents to write: "The wages are regulated on the one hand by a natural law; their minimum is determined by the physical minimum required by the laborer for the conservation of his labor-power and for its reproduction —;" but "historically developed social needs"[6] help to fix this minimum. So far the author of "Capital," to which may be added Engels' stress of the opposite viewpoint that "the underconsumption of the masses is a necessary condition of all forms of society in which robbers and robbed exist, and therefore of the capitalist system."[7] The difficulty of harmonizing these two contentions must have been apparent to Marx, but it is never candidly acknowledged.

But if labor is the sole fount of wealth land is not generically different from capital. This is the point brought out by Marx, as a result of which he again takes issue with Ricardo. For he now grants to land a share for the same reason that he also favors the capitalist. Rent, too, is part of the loot legalized by the private property régime. Rent is plunder precisely in the same sense that profits

[6] Marx, K., *ibidem,* vol. 3, p. 1000; or vol. 1, pp. 189–190.
[7] Engels, F., "Anti-Dühring."

were. Capitalist and landlord were two of a kind. Neither was acting honestly. However, unlike Ricardo who pointed his accusing finger at the landlord, Marx was chiefly intent upon exposing the trickery of the capitalist. Industry had grown since Ricardian days. The city worker was everywhere in evidence. It seemed natural to bring the offending industrialist to justice first, and to let the minor culprit go free for a while. In a sense, the socialists had to admit, the landlord was the spoiled darling of mother nature, just as the classic economists had themselves believed.

But what of the employment of capital and labor in its effects upon profits, particularly upon the rate of profit? Marx got into difficulties, as is well known, because his labor theory of value left no room for the productiveness of machinery. The employer raised his profits as he increased the number of laborers engaged. This agreed with Marxian theories and should have prevented the movements of the dividend, that is of profits which the market recorded. Some critics of Marx have maintained that by this test alone the labor notion of price fell down completely, since facts contradicted it constantly. Either price and profits were not solely dependent on labor, or the Marxian analysis failed to take care of one problem in distribution. The harm, however, was not as great as may appear. For if Marx had insisted that, while labor was the sole source of value, it was only one factor combining with capital goods for purposes of production, he would have been safe. The varying ratios of capital and labor in a productive act need then not have bothered him so much. The decisive factor would still have been labor, though its alliance with capital was a condition of productiveness usually, if not always. But for that matter the case was not nearly so much of a test for socialistic philosophy as has been affirmed by its most outspoken enemies. The Marxian system is not shaken by confessions of error in pricing schemes. Nothing great was at stake. Marx knew that the rate of profits varied with the volume of capital used,[8] and remembering it he could admit it without renouncing his labor theory of value.

The Marxian viewpoint is in other respects self-consistent like the Ricardian which he combats. He believed that a rising share of the national income had to go to land and capital. This followed naturally from the surplus notion which pictured the laborer as receiving only what was necessary to reproduce his labor power, while the excess of time he worked yielded products stolen by the owner of capital who thus accumulated huge sums, until finally a catastrophe would overtake him. But of this more in a later chapter.

It is worth while to point to the distinction between the *percentage* of the aggregate social income accruing to labor or capital, and the *rate* of profits or wages. The latter refers to what the average capitalist or wage earner gets, the former would mean the share known as profits or wages distributed among all the capitalists or workers respectively. As others had long pointed out: According to the Malthusian principle the labor contingent increases and their total food wages may rise, but the income of each laborer in foodstuffs cannot rise, and may shrink. Similarly in the Marxian position. The average laborer has no prospect of improving his lot, though there will be a growing number of laborers claiming an absolutely larger amount in wages. Only, Ricardo

[8] "Die Profitrate nimmt ab im Verhaltnis zur steigenden Akkumulation des Kapitals, und der ihr entsprechenden steigenden Produktivkraft der gesellschaftlichen Arbeit"; in "Capital," vol. 3, p. 384. But see also pp. 193 & 199.

thought that owing to technical improvements the laborer would benefit somewhat in the end by gaining on enterprise, even if he paid tribute to the landlord. Marx could not agree to this concession, and drove his premises to their ultimate conclusion. Marx consequently had to cast about for other means to save the masses.

That under such circumstances he could not love the competitive spirit goes without saying; however, he professed to like it because its continuance and unhampered sway would precipitate the proletarian revolt. This was the nature of his tolerance toward Laissez Faire. He would vote for it and for free trade since it tended naturally to destroy individualism. It was, therefore, a good thing to espouse.[9] But Ricardo preached Laissez Faire because he argued from promises first laid down by Adam Smith, the acceptance of which inevitably led to conclusions out of accord with state interference.

As will be seen from Table One the two philosophies agree in only eight out of the eighteen points specified. The departures on the part of Marx from the classic system are more marked than his agreements with it, and the practical consequences are poles asunder.

§ 4. **Criticism of Marxian Economics.**— What is to be said in regard to the position which Marx defended so strenuously during his lifetime and which since then has often been restated by his followers?

In the first place, evidently, the Marxian analysis can no longer satisfy us because the facts go against it. The lot of the average man has been improved instead of going from bad to worse as Marx predicted. He has more to spend and has a greater variety of goods to consume than a few generations ago. The level of living has risen per-

9 In a speech delivered on Jan. 1 1849, in Brussels on "Die Lage des Freihandels."

Table One

A Comparison of Marxian ~~with Ricardian~~ and Marginal Economics

Ricardo	*Marx*	*Marginists*
1. Private property is assumed.	1 Private property is incompatible with socialized production.	1. Private property is assumed.
2. Utility is the power of gratifying any want.	2 Utility is the power of gratifying any want.	2. Utility is the power of gratifying any want.
3. Goods are scarce (transfer able) utilities.	3 Goods are scarce (transferable) utilities.	3. Goods are scarce (transferable) utilities.
4. Value is an exchange ratio of goods.	4 Value is an exchange ratio of goods.	4. Value is an exchange ratio of goods.
5. Capital is wealth used productively.	5 Capital legally is a monopoly in production goods; but intrinsically it is the product of labor, a kind of solidified labor.	5. Capital is wealth used productively.
6. Price is naturally fixed by labor cost, excepting some non-reproducibles and machinofactures.	6 Price is naturally fixed by socially necessary labor cost, monopolies excepted.	6. Price, excepting monopolies, is measured by equalized marginal valuations expressed in supply and demand.
7. Cost is labor spent by the individual in producing goods.	7 Cost is labor spent by the average worker in production.	7. Cost is the sum of efforts, expenses are loss of values.
8. There are three producing agents.	8 There is only one producing agent, capital and land being mere rights to labor's product.	8. There are four producing agents (factors).
9. Productivity is a competitive concept.	9 Productivity should be socialized.	9. Productivity is a competitive concept.

Ricardo	Marx	Marginists
10. Agriculture is subject to the law of diminishing returns, other investments not.	Agriculture is subject to the law of diminishing returns, other labor not.	10. All production is subject to the law of the proportionality of factors.
11. Malthusianism is a fundamental physical law.	Malthusianism is a law to be offset by proper distribution.	11. Malthusianism is a tendency to be offset by birth-control.
12. The price of labor approximates a subsistence wage.	Wages tend to equal the cost of producing labor-power.	12. The price of labor and capital tends to equal their marginal product.
13. The price of the use of land is the supra-marginal product.	The price of the use of land is the supra-marginal product.	13. The price of the use of land is the supra-marginal product.
14. The price of enterprise (capital) is a residual, labor and land being paid first, according to physical laws.	The price of the use of capital (enterprise) is the difference between the price and the product of labor-power.	14. The price of enterprise is, under perfect competition, mere wages (of management), and in any case a residual claim.
15. Progress gives a growing share of the social product to labor and land.	Progress gives a growing share of the social product to land and capital.	15. Progress gives a growing share of the social product to land and capital.
16. The rate of rent rises, while that of profits falls.	The rate of rent rises, while that of profits and interest will fall.	16. The rate of rent and wages rises, while that of interest and profits falls.
17. Competition is a law of nature.	Competition will be superseded by socialism.	17. Competition is a law of nature.
18. Laissez Faire ensures maximum wealth and welfare.	Laissez Faire is desirable because it will hasten the advent of socialism.	18. Laissez Faire, with some exceptions, ensures maximum wealth and welfare.

ceptibly, and the middle class, so far from dying out, has increased numerically. True, the bulk of the population even in the most progressive countries is still working under contract, the capitalist having usually the upper hand in the bargaining, but this has not prevented labor from obtaining a goodly part of the improvements enjoyed by the wealthy. Cycles of booms and depressions have recurred as before, but exploitation has not grown in proportion, as Marxian economics taught. If all, or even the major portion, of what labor produces above a bare subsistence fund, had gone to capital the misery of the multitude would be infinitely greater than it is.

In the second place, the theory of surplus value becomes logically untenable when competition between laborers, due to the complete mobility of labor which it assumes, ends. One cannot accept this thesis of ruthless exploitation without imagining the individual worker left entirely to his own resources, deserted by his mates and betrayed by a plutocratic government. But this sort of mobility never existed, as even Adam Smith was anxious to admit for all his belief in individualism. Human nature is often stronger than legal provisions for freedom of contract and of residence. People become addicted to habits. They develop a fondness for places and memories. They will not move, though offered a higher wage. Also, they have since the rise of socialism learned to combine. The right of association has not been denied them. The union has done away with the advantage that men of means, and particularly of the means of production, used to have, or reputedly had, in bargaining with labor. A new method of pricing has arisen that is a long way removed from the facts of competition and mobility which the classics pictured.

In the third place capital is not solidified labor, because matter is not altogether the same as mind. Motion is not notion. True, we do well in tracing mental phenomena by their physiological equivalents. The plan of the scientist to ascertain the nature of mental states by forms of behavior objectively measurable is not a contemptible one. The physical correlatives are ordinarily there to be studied. They enable us to determine the routine of reactions in man, which otherwise might remain undecipherable. But this does not mean the identification of quantity and quality. Generic differences between mind and matter should be granted to exist unless special purposes forbid.

So, by the same token, it is an error to call machines mere material put together by a working hand. Work for the economist is not what it is to the physicist. The physicist defines work as the overcoming of resistance through space. He is interested in actions and reactions. He deals with quantities only. The social student, on the contrary, is primarily engrossed in questions of value. Values are the subject matter particularly of economics. And values originate in scarcity, whatever amount of energy is needed to change the forms of matter.

Goods represent ideas. They are the embodiment of thoughts infinitely rare at one time, and made cheap only in the course of social evolution. All labor, to illustrate our point, may be divided into the repetitive and the innovating kind. The former may be quantitatively measured. It suggests comparisons. If, for instance, I plow now one acre, and the next time two acres, using the same tools and methods, I have added to value and may anticipate an increased return. But I have created nothing new. I get more wheat, but it is of the same sort. I used more implements, but of the same sort. Everything was repetition or multiplication. But suppose I breed a new variety of wheat, suppose I make certain alterations in the plow-share, suppose I change my principle of fertilizing the soil. Here we have an innovation that leads to distinct products: Perhaps it is a new sort of wheat, or wheat in larger amounts for constant effort.

There is a reliable test for invention or innovation. Namely, if with constant effort, thanks to changes in capital or in the use of it, I procure a bigger return, then I have been an inventor. Or, if I create a new article, something not heretofore on the market, then again I have shown inventiveness. All things now familiar were new once upon a time. There is hardly anything on the market but it was invented once. If an article becomes cheaper or is improved, that change means an innovation in the economic sense.

Considering these objective tests for an innovation we have an excellent way for distinguishing between things and thoughts. In a printing press we have a combination of thoughts that may or may not have cost effort-in-time. It is not always easy to say when or how an idea originated. In general, to be sure, ideas are the fruit of much intellectual toil. We must have so much schooling and technical training, whether it's as novelists or as chemists or as mechanics. There is work back of invention. But at the moment a thought comes it may not involve a time-element of labor. Effort-in-time is the sort of effort spent in digging a ditch. We see the motions and may measure them by the hands on the dial of a watch. So with most repetitive acts producing wealth. Yet this is not so applicable to inspirations resulting in new products or in cheapening methods. What shall we say of the inventor of rod and reel, of Arabic numbers, of the alphabet, of the steam engine, or of whatever innovation in science or economics we may have in mind? These are the result of immeasurable labors.

Ideas are rare, and therefore fetch a high price. It was a good principle for Marx to demand the socialization of ideas, but a bad one to put all sorts of labor into a single class. "Socially necessary labor" is a concept as inadequate as we know the concept of averages to be. Innovations and repetitions should not be put on a level. They are incomparable. Capital goods are not labors piled up in a heap, to be assembled and taken apart at command. The funding of all labor varieties was an awkward scheme for determining price, which after all was not Marx's main task.

Let us put the matter in another way by asking what would become of the surplus if innovation ever ceased. Marx declares that by making the laborer work for longer hours than are needed to supply him with the essentials of life the capitalist reaps a rich harvest. It is said he takes the extra hours' product and uses it to employ more labor to continue his unfair practices. Thus he waxes rich, and labor is cheated of its belongings. One is tempted to give ear to the argument, were it not for the accumulation of the surplus. If at the beginning this surplus is wheat, what do we use it for? The answer can not be that it is to employ more labor to cultivate more land so as to produce more wheat. For, in the first place, this is not the record of economic achievements, and in the second place it does not appeal to our sense of proportions. Ere long we should have enormous stocks of wheat; but what for? It is easy to provide for a rainy day, and it is natural to hoard some things. But an endless accumulation of one commodity does not help much. The end of life is variation. The spice of life is variety. The march of progress is toward diversification. Ever new things, this is the motto: not an excess of some one staple like wheat. A surplus, originally of foods perhaps, could be valuable only if part of it were used to feed men, not to till the fields to produce wheat, but to produce another kind of food product, or more likely something not to eat, but to wear. And later on each year's surplus of a given class of goods should serve only to dedicate energy to new endeavors. An increase of labor is necessary for the diversification of products. Growth of population is neither an end, nor always an incident, in economic progress. Not multiplication of men and materials, not this primarily, but diversification of products is the chief aim. A larger number of goods produced at less cost!

What is the moral? This, that exploitation in itself could not help the captialists if they were not assured of new methods and new products, that is of ideas, of inventions which might have been their own, or the laborer's. The surplus view of Marx must either recognize classes of work distinct in a value analysis, or it preaches a silly accumulation of goods that nobody wants because they would soon exceed all possible needs.

But, in the fourth place, value itself is not measurable by the amount of labor spent in its creation. That follows from what has just been said. But it also is shown by everyday experience, and besides, it was admitted by Marx. Marx indeed had two ways of stating his attitude. He could say: Under competitive individualism value is determined by something else than labor cost. True, but I disapprove it. And he could argue: Under socialism prices will vary with costs as defined, that is with socially necessary labor. The latter is the only correct pricing principle. But as we know, Marx did not commit himself in that manner. Instead he pictured prices as labor results quantitatively measurable and comparable, while insisting also upon a standard of living which according to his surplus theory of value did not exist under capitalism. That under socialism as well as on present terms costs of labor cannot always fix values appears at first moment, but Marx thought the exception to his rule inconsequential.

§ 5. **Marginal Economics.**— The Marxian economics should be taken seriously and hence criticized where modern science urges it. But it is easy to belittle the Marxian concept without remembering its great merits and the influence it has wielded over later minds. More particularly one may make sport of some Marxian notions, forgetting that our current economic viewpoint does not rise much above them. The group of economists who stood out in arms against the socialists also attacked the historical movement in general, and of course they had increasingly occasion to revise the classic version to Smith, Senior, Ricardo, and of the two Mills. The prevailing economics, though no longer as homogeneous as at the opening of this century, is therefore a reaction against both Ricardianism and against historism. The hope of deducting permanent principles from an exhaustive searching into economic history has been pretty well abandoned. A number of factors contributed to the decline of the historical methods, though we may regard J. S. Mill's Logis, which appeared in 1842, as a turning point for economic method; for Mill's own Principles of Economics show no trace of a method distinctive of social science, as presaged in the Logic. If the acute J. S. Mill returned to deduction, what could others expect from historism? The Austrian economists combated historism because of their training under philosophers who separated rigidly deduction from induction, and had no confidence in Hegelian prophecies. Hence men like Menger and Wieser, Boehm-Bawerk and Sax were ready to reclaim the field of investigation, which the Historical School, like scientific socialism, had declared barren and unfit for use.

But in fact, the marginal approach was in thorough agreement with the psychological movement of the second and third quarters of the nineteenth century. The trend was distinctly toward introspective analysis supplemented and corrected by exact measurement of reactions to externally applied stimuli. Psychology rapidly established itself as an objective science, with the result that the facts of human nature were definitely classified and characterized.

This way of redefining values marks also the marginal school of economists who, beginning with Gossen, Walras, and Jevons, revamped the Ricardian notions by shifting the emphasis from work to wants, and from materials to margins of response. Much of the classic structure was left untouched, but the nomenclature changed greatly.

The marginal viewpoint abandoned the attempt of explaining prices through expenses in time and effort. It went directly to the question of wants, and by comparing their different intensities tried to explain prices. It showed that we care relatively the less for a stock of goods the larger it is, and that we constantly seek to equalize our supplies of different kinds of commodities. Hence the marginal procedure led away from costs to sacrifice, and from production of stuffs to creation of values, no matter whether they took palpable form or not.

Like the Ricardian the marginal view is static. It pictures a process at rest in a given moment, much as a photograph reveals certain facial expressions. The advantages of a moving picture over a snapshot compare approximately with the superiorities of a dynamic over a static method of dissection.

Like Ricardo, the Marginists, too, assume competition, private property, and freedom of contract. It is not for them to question the worth of our social order. They take it as it is and proceed to define their terms accordingly. Everything hinges on competition and on the mobility of labor and capital. Since, furthermore, capital is a right under the law it is entitled to a share of the national product. But here the Marginists became bold in making out of capital goods a bundle of property rights rather than a work of ideas. Rights were continually stressed, and social aspects subordinated to them. Capital, even if not taking concrete shape, they called a factor of production just as truly as manual labor or soil fertility. There existed consequently at least three "factors" of production, though toward the end of the century enterprise was segregated from labor upon due recognition of its unique functions under individualism. Thus we get really four agents in production, all of which had a share in the social dividend according to some principle of distribution.

The notion of cost was materially modified, for as against the classics the Marginists did not begin with labor. They started with desires. They asked: Why is so much labor spent in producing an article, and instead of answering as the older men would have, that the technique of production could not do it in less time, they pointed to the intensity of our want. Man, it now appeared, was willing to give so much labor to the creation of a certain commodity because compared with others he wanted it so much that the labor did not seem excessive. The need of food, shelter, and clothing comes first. Nothing can take precedence over it, and hence any amount of toil necessary to produce them will be expended. But for the remainder of our level of living we are governed by different rates of wants, some being intense enough to follow immediately after the essentials, and others being classed as luxuries. The march of progress is the extension of wants and the thinning of the margins at which we choose to buy one article instead of another. When we have decided on this matter, then the amount of effort devoted to the production of an article will be revealed. Costs are the proof of valuation measured by our willingness to sacrifice one good for another. Time and energy, materials and thought, are secondary facts in the explanation of price.

The whole subject of cost versus want was finally worked over and the true relation between the two disclosed. It could hardly escape the notice of observant students that expenses as treated by the marginal view were valuations of the past, and that therefore in a sense all costs were values. But by the same ruling expenses could be admitted as a certain objective way of measuring subjective aspects, and so, in stretching the static outlook to cover decades at a time, costs and wants became complementary. "In the long run" they could be pictured as two sides of one and the same thing. The reconciliation seemed opportune, and served to give a new lease of life to the individualistic conception of product and price.

As shown in our Table, productivity according to the Marginists is a rate of return in goods per outgo of other goods, each good being defined as a scarce transferable utility, and a utility as *anything satisfying any* want. From this followed the interesting development of the concept of diminishing returns which no Ricardian would have understood. It was shown that since production is a competitive concept referring to values, the costs of production could not fall merely in agriculture. For one thing, the yield in concrete things did not mean everything because economics reckons in values, in dollars and cents. If the farmer, for instance, sold a smaller crop at a larger aggregate gain than a larger crop in the previous year, then his rate of return had risen. And in the next place it became more and more apparent that in all fields of endeavor there is a right and a wrong way of doing things. The terrifying law of diminishing returns thus was converted into the perfectly harmless principle of a proportionality of factors. It was shown, as everybody indeed knew, that temperance is a virtue, that a sense of proportions will do wonders, that too much of one element in a compound will spoil it. The marginal view made land, labor, capital and enterprise the four factors of production. Let them be mixed in one way, and maximum return results for the business manager; let him violate the law of proportions and he will obtain less than the maximum. Space and time also entered into the situation, and all in all the purification of Ricardian notions left the economist little better off than he had been before.

But the marginal definition of productivity helped in one respect. Namely the rule of margins in valuation was applied to the services of the agents in production, the rate of pay depending on the marginal product of each agent. On a short-time view the least effectively employed unit of labor or capital set the pace for the remaining units. None could get more than the marginal one, for the same reason that the least valued dose in a stock of homogeneous goods fixed the value of the whole stock. One had only to multiply the number of units in a stock by the utility — or value — of the marginal item to compute the value of the whole stock. Incomes varied on the same principle. On a long-time view however the better worker was a blessing to the inferior, for competition would sooner or later force a distribution of the additional product, the marginal man benefiting with the rest. Each factor received his "product" as per definition. Profits were the only exception, because they tended toward a minimum. Or rather, as some announced, there were no profits under perfect competition, only a wage of management.

Consequently land and labor benefited most by technical improvements. Interest rates were also subject to the general law, but meant less to the practical-minded student of distribution. Laborers would obtain a growing share of the national dividend because of the effect of invention on productivity. The landlord could not claim it all, as Ricardo had apprehended. The economic process was less cruel than the classics had made it out to be. Hence the Marginists favored frankly the competitive principle and tolerated interference only where it was proven absolutely indispensable. They had shown that each gets what he deserves according to definitions of utility, value, and capital, so no occasion arose for complaint.

A glance at Table One informs us that the marginal and the Ricardian viewpoints are not as far apart as either compared with the socialistic. In spite of important revisions the Ricardian doctrine survived the advent of Marginism. The modern orthodox economic standpoint marks a step in advance, but its logic is the old. The competitive principle colors everything. Abstractions rule as before. Ricardo like the Marginists approved of the world as he found it. As the Table shows they agreed in nine out of the eighteen points, while Marx and the Marginists had only five in common. Four of the eighteen points were held in common by Ricardians, Marxians, and Marginists, but of course Marx's definitions of value are only provisional. He is opposed to the individualistic norms. He uses them solely to arraign the capitalist. His chief aim is the annihilation of what the other two groups wished to leave undisturbed.

The question then is not merely one of logic. One will ask: How much more satisfactory was the marginal view than the heresies of socialism? Or, more to the point, what oddities of reasoning appear in it that orthodox economics is not guilty of, too?

§ 6. **Criticism of Marginal Economics.**—The Marxian like the Ricardian view emphasizes labor as the source of values, and it measures them by the amounts of labor spent in the creation of a value. This is one way of making values objective and is naturally thought of first because time and effort are facts every one is acquainted with. Marx saw no reason for rejecting the labor standard, though he enlarged upon the concept by socializing labor. He not only proposed to attribute all values in exchange to the labor needed for the production of scarce utilities, but he furthermore averaged different rates of production. He made three points: He declared labor to be the sole fount of all values; he reduced all kinds of effort, manual and mental, to a homogeneous stock (what he called labor power) and he standardized costs in labor by establishing an arithmetical average of different amounts of labor applied, in terms of hours of work, by different individuals or groups to the production of equal values. This latter procedure was peculiarly Marxian.

Now, the marginal procedure is different in one sense,

but much like it in another, for while it displaces labor by valuations, it none the less averages different valuations just as Marx averaged different productivities measured by effort-in-time. According to the marginal view different want intensities of different individuals with different tastes and different incomes, that is purchasing powers, may be reduced to an average which expresses itself in the bidding of buyers and sellers in a competitive market. It has been pointed out by critics that such is not an admissible device, because logically no such average can be proven to exist. Individuals as averages are a piece of fiction anyway. But it deserves mention here that the marginal economists made this average a central feature in their price determination.

What is more, the Marxian assumption of a fairly constant labor-power per average individual has the advantage of making one cost do for several sales at different times. But if the Marginists are right, valuations fluctuate constantly so that really an article is sold at a valuation of the present moment which in all probability differs from the valuations embodied in the article *at the time it was produced.* That is, we must resort to another averaging of variations of want in order to establish some fixed relation between the price of a finished commodity, which by the way represents as many prices as it has constituent costs, and the productivity-rate of return. To the Marginists this relation is a very definite one. It is one of identity. Prices measure factorial shares. But the averaging is as risky for the productivity-theory of incomes as it is inadequate for the explanation of commodity prices.

Marx was not so embarrassed, for in adopting implicitly, though not expressedly, the Malthusian formula he simplified distribution as Ricardo had done. There were only three factors. One was paid a subsistence wage, the other received a supra-marginal product from the soil, and the third took the leavings. Very simple!

The marginal standpoint, however, led to other predicaments, some of them not more amusing than impressive. For instance, according to the concept of consumer's surplus a man saved the more the less he saved. In the great majority of cases a purchase was a saving because the article was worth more to the buyer than he was forced under competition to pay for it. He had all kinds of units of utility left after he got his money's worth. Let him, therefore, spend more and enjoy more consumer's surplus.

On the other hand there was the bugbear of alternative costs which no entrepreneur could escape. He was rarely sure of having invested his funds the best possible way. Every advantage in employment of capital was offset by the sacrifice of investment elsewhere. The option was a nagging thought that should figure in the ledger when investment was not the most lucrative possible. A farmer too should reckon as costs for fodder the price at which he would have had to buy it hadn't he produced it himself at a lower cost. And the interest charge grew every minute, for everything reconvertible into pure capital, or what once was in the shape of liquid capital, ate up interest. All consumption goods, indeed, *might* have been used as capital. Since they were not, a loss could be claimed. The individualistic outlook permitted such cost accounting.

It also gave birth to the famous paradox of value which the Austrian economists first expounded, and which has often since served to illustrate the principle of marginal utilities. But note what one might flippantly infer from it: It apparently makes it possible to destroy and create capital in the same act. If the spice-importers, for instance, feared the effect of large supplies on price they could save themselves by sinking a portion of the cargo of spices. They would sink the ships and raise the prices and probably aggregate profits. Such is the test of monopoly. They used the cargo as part of their working capital, say of their "circulating" capital. They destroyed part of this capital by casting spices overboard. But the same act also increased the value of the residual of spices. Capital was therefore created while it was destroyed.

Or notice the curiosity of the marginal capital definition, by which one and the same article became alternately capital and non-capital, that is a consumption good. The piano in the baker's shop was capital while used to attract customers. It was part of his earning assets then. But if used to entertain the same people after closing hours it became a mere utility. The baker's family listened to an instrument forming part of his wages of management; the customers were regaled by the employment of capital. Likewise cocaine sold illicitly at a drugstore was capital, while mother's care of her children was non-productive labor, since it was not offered for sale in the open market.

Finally, it deserves mention that Marx was at least consistent in his position as ethicist. He did better than the marginal group for two reasons. Namely, in the first place he did not incorporate moral topics in his Capital. True, like his followers, he hinted plainly at a moral issue. Nobody could condemn private capital and not plead guilty to a charge of moralism. But Marx kept reform programs out of his text. He did not profess to purge economics of all ethical background and then proceed to discuss at great length many questions of reform and legislation such as frequently characterize modern texts for school use.

In the second place he grounded his ethics more securely than the Marginists who were drilled in the metaphysical style of moralizing. If economics declines to deal with moral matters, pretending that somebody else has preëmpted that field, it is guilty of a contradiction of terms. It was socialism which first drove home this point, and familiarized the man of the street with the social aspects of religion and ethics. The Marxian economics excels in that it makes ethics part of social science. It reduces all knowledge to experience, that of the moralist included. Largely to demonstrate this unity of thought and to give reform movements a solid basis the founders of socialism elaborated their concept of history, thus preparing the way for a view of life which must unify all sciences, however distinct their subjects.

CHAPTER III

THE ECONOMIC INTERPRETATION OF HISTORY

§ 1. **Main Roots of the Economic Interpretation of History.**— Back of Marx's " Kapital " is his economic interpretation of history. It is hardly possible to understand fully what he meant to say in his ponderous economic treatise without looking into his other views of a somewhat philosophic nature. In regard to Marx we have here a situation that not infrequently is true of other great minds. We read one of their works and judge them by it, or at least consider it something complete in itself, forgetting that, if more was written, it probably bears on the very book we are studying. For mind is a unit, and eminent thinkers have given perspective to their thought so that what appears at one place is more or less closely connected with everything else. As we grow we frequently change our interests and write on subjects originally not at all in our mind. We are driven from one problem to another, and so ultimately arrive at ideas that will influence us the rest of our life in treating of anything, no matter how far apart the topics. Thus it is difficult to appreciate Aristotle's " Politics " unless one is familiar with his Metaphysics and Ethics. Thus we may read Adam Smith on the " Wealth of Nations," but fail to get its total range without some knowledge of his " Theory of the Moral Sentiments." Thus again one is entitled to judge John Stuart Mill by his " Principles of Political Economy." That work should stand or fall by its contents. But how much may easily be missed if his "Logic" has not been given a thorough inspection beforehand!

And so with Marx and Engels as founders of socialism. Their criticism of the individualistic economics of their day is one thing. We may understand it and draw our conclusions. But what Marx said in his "Kapital," and how he said it, that is a point to be inquired into by an independent study of his earlier expositions on history and Hegelianism. Huge growths have remote beginnings. Giant trees send out their main roots deep into the soil, and far from the trunk feeders are still to be found whose function is to give life to the very trunk that seems so majestically self-sufficient. Great rivers similarly have their headwaters in perhaps far off, inaccessible regions. In lofty heights the stream is born that later on we find so useful and overpowering in its grandeur. We do not possibly care to explore the upper reaches, but in this distant ancestry that gives rise to so many tributaries we have the explanation of the end result itself.

The founders of socialism were no mean men. They were extraordinary men who worked like titans and pierced the surface of things. They went far for their raw material out of which the socialistic creed was slowly built. They consulted many sources and drew inspiration from thinkers that in their time had no interest in matters economic. Thus the intellectual labors of preceding centuries bore fruit in the controversial writings of Marx and Engels, and in their propaganda which since has given so much food for thought to an inquiring age. One must read Marx's articles in the *Rheinische Zeitung*, or his books against Proudhon and the Feuerbach group, to divine some of the thoughts basic to socialism. In his

"Misery of Philosophy" and "Holy Family" are elements reconstructed later in the "Critique of Political Economy," but utilized also in the "Communist Manifesto," as well as in the "Kapital." Of Engels the output is in a sense not so important because it was for the most part written after the economic interpretation of history had been formulated. Yet there is much of value in the "Anti-Dühring" and in the "Essay on Feuerbach," both of which represent answers to critics of scientific socialism as it flourished in the last quarter of the nineteenth century. Engels was the philosopher, if Marx was the economist. However, on the one hand, Marx could think philosophically himself, though he had done with it comparatively early in life, and on the other hand Engels never forgot the economic background whose disagreeable features had prompted him to describe the condition of the working classes in England, as they existed in the second quarter of his century. Strictly speaking both were incapable of the sort of thinking which characterizes professional philosophers. We do not find any evidence that they could follow Hegel, e. g., through the maze of his reasoning which led from "Logic" to the "Philosophy of History." In perusing the youthful works of Marx one is struck with what he didn't notice in Hegel rather than with what he selected for criticism. However, while he made no pretense of fathoming the full depth of metaphysical problems, he took care to seize upon salient points that could prove useful to his sociological outlook. Hence the transcendental thought of Hegel's time is part of scientific socialism. Hence the "Critique of Political Economy" really begins with searchings into matters not now recognized as scientific.

Whether the economic interpretation of history is peculiarly the product of Marx and Engels is perhaps not an important question. Those who have delved somewhat into the genesis of that mighty concept will probably concede to the founders of socialism a large measure of originality in this respect. One may make many excursions into the relevant literature of those days without meeting any such formula as Marx and Engels made famous in their "Manifesto of 1848." On the whole it seems fair to grant these two men the lion share of the glory, and to distinguish generously between the ingredients they found at hand and the product they turned out with them. There had been materialism before, as everybody knows, but it had not been given a historical application. There had been economic interpretations of life from the early eighteenth century on, but they had not been cloaked in a metaphysical form. Historiography is of ancient origin, and the notion of change dates from early Greek speculation, but none of it yielded a Marxian recipe.

Again, the genetic standpoint which socialism has always so ardently defended predominated when Marx was born. The Romantic movement was essentially genetic. One looked back to forget the present, or to understand it. The great names of that age are known as well for their views on the social process as for their literary creations. But, once more, this does not rob Marx and Engels of their supreme merit as first expounders of a materialistic view of history.

We might say: England is the cradle of materialism as the metaphysician understands the term. From there it went to France and gave rise to a school of thought whose culminating achievement is, in a way, the Méchanique Celeste of La Place. The writings of Cabanis and Diderot and Helvetius familiarized people with a materialistic valuation of life. The Baron d'Holbach also contributed his mite. But this type of materialism was too mechanical to suit Marx. Like Engels he relied more upon Hobbes and Locke than upon the French. On the other hand, the historical viewpoint had gained ground notably in France. Lamarck and Condorcet were great figures. And again, if from England came Spencer, Darwin, and Wallace, Germany furnished a Herder, Humboldt and Goethe. Thus three countries provided the streams of thought that finally converged in the socialistic movement. The biological aspect is English, the historical aspect first gained repute in France, and the sociological or economic aspect was most cultivated in Germany. Together these nations developed the evolutionary standpoint. Thanks to such beginnings the socialists could go ahead. Hegel completed for Marx what Hobbes and Montesquieu had begun.

The German materialistic view of Büchner and his ilk was of no great moment for Marx. It came somewhat too late. Furthermore, Marx wanted concepts of motion, not pronouncements on matter or space. The achievements of chemistry therefore did not greatly impress him as a student in quest of a masterkey which should open the doors to social progress. The inclination for a matter of fact view of life existed early in him no less than in Engels, but the impetus that moved him onward till death came from the last of the philosophic critics! Hegel "made" Marx!

§ 2. **Influence of Hegel.**— It is of no import here what Hegel preached and how he reacted upon the "Critique of Pure Reason." But we must keep in mind some of the main tenets on which he erected his phenomenal reputation as a metaphysician. Hegel was a Platonian absolutist, for one thing. In the second place his analysis of mind and knowledge led him to the evolving of a concept of progress and reality which is unique in philosophic history. Hegel not only believed in a reality transcending our sense experience, but he pictured the processes of cognition as focussed upon a single point which marked the terminal of social evolution. To Hegel there was a design in history. The teleological assumption pervades all his reasoning. And with this he coupled a theory of State that has astonished those who dwell fondly on his Logic. Hegel, then, was a theist with monarchical leanings, an exponent of idealistic values, and a firm believer in the scientific character of introspection, of what he called the science of all sciences, to wit Logic.

Marx was not enamored with this side of the great teacher at Berlin. But he, like Engels, took readily to the other side in Hegelian teachings which later on gave rise to diverse empirical movements in philosophy. Hegel namely sought to establish the identity of nature and mind in a manner not attempted by Kant. He bore in mind more consistently than his illustrious predecessors the maxim that whatever we know is limited by a knower. Intelligibility rests on the intelligence, and to look beyond this is a task distinct from the first principles in logic. The first principles must seek to explain how we know anything and how our experiences may change without losing continuity. This problem drove Hegel to his dialectic by which he connected the object with the subject. He admitted that in reflecting upon our experiences we actually alter their contents, but he also pointed to the connecting link between steps of cognition. We do get ahold of the world about us, though our conclusions change as we shift viewpoint and alter premises. A contrasting and compounding of judgments ever takes place. By it we secure new truths, but move in pendulum swings that turn truth into falsehood. We go from thesis to antithesis, and hence to synthesis. In an Aufhebung der Momente, as Hegel styles the process, we add to our knowledge while losing part of what we have felt. Thus, logically viewed, learning is given movement and direction. All things become relative. We live in a world of contradictions. What the old logicians said about laws of Identity and Excluded Middle is only under certain reservations acceptable, for a thing may both be and not be. It may be good and bad also. If it *is* not, it may become. If it *is*, there exists a raison d'être, but as against this we have the prospect of decay and a resurrection of the old in totally different forms.

This idea that all things are relative to each in the sense that one judgment necessarily grows out of a preceding one — a thought Hegel seems to have distilled from studies in Greek metaphysics — this idea suited the temperament and needs of Marx and Engels. They poked fun at the absolutistic phase of Hegelian beliefs, but they were deeply impressed with the weight of his main contention.

When Hegel wrote that "the State represents God's progress in the world, it rests on the power of will taking embodiment in Reason. The State must not be identified with any particular nation, but with God himself" [1] — Marx could not give assent. As early as 1843 he suggests that "the worst enemy of real humanism (that is of socialism) in Germany is speculative idealism." [2] And in the "Holy Family" Feuerbach is lauded because he put Man in the place of "all this folderol about the in-

[1] Hegel, "Enzyklopædie," § 258; § 272.

[2] Marx, K., "Heilige Familie," Preface, printed in Mehring, F. Aus dem Literarischen Nachlass von Karl Marx, Friedrich Engels, und Ferdinand Lassalle, Volume I.

finite self-consciousness,"[3] which Hegel made the center of his Logic. Idealism was not to the liking of men who were engrossed in economic studies and sought a remedy for existing evils. More particularly Marx was not satisfied with the type of historism he read out of the Enzyklopædie. He exclaims: "Hegel's historical concept is nothing but a speculative expression of the Christian-Teutonic dogma of opposition between spirit and matter, between God and the world."[4] Such a construction was alien, perhaps, to the mind of a converted Jew.

But all the more glad, then, were the founders of scientific socialism when after Hegel's death one group of disciples turned radical and exploited the relativistic side rather than the idealistic. Hegel's immense range and generalizing applications admitted naturally of a great variety of interpretations. Those who saw the force of the first and second part of his Logic agreed to ignore the third, thus getting rid of absolutism. The pragmatic penchant in the master was now boldly emphasized and quickly elaborated into a new sort of humanism. We have men who like the brothers Feuerbach, like Bauer and Strauss transferred the logical relativity into a sociological one. Feuerbach especially created a stir with his "Essence of Christianity" in which religion was humanized and Christianity expounded in metaphysical fashion. In the end Ludwig Feuerbach turned away from the materialistic position that at first his readers placed him in, but Marx kept what he found good and used it for his historical interpretation.

Hegel himself had furnished part of the Marxian view, as was frankly admitted. As Engels at a later date put it: "From this (the Hegelian) point of view the history

[3] *Ibidem,* Chapter VI.
[4] *Ibidem,* Chapter V.

of mankind no longer appeared as a wild whirl of senseless deeds of violence, all equally condemnable at the judgment seat of mature philosophic reason, as deeds which are best forgotten, but as the process of evolution of man himself. It was now the task of the intellect to follow the gradual march of this process through all its devious ways, and to trace out the inner law running through all its apparently accidental phenomena."[5] And when Feuerbach added to this the humanistic concept by which man was made the center of things, the sole judge and jury of all values in science and philosophy, then historism assumed definite meaning. The hedonistic view of Friedrich Feuerbach prevailed over the theism of his elder brother.[6]

Hegel's devotion to an Absolute was ridiculed. His transcendentalism evoked only the scorn of Marx who concluded that the metaphysical procedure turned things upside down, making a phantom out of what was real, and worshipful truth out of what man had known and never could sense. To Hegel, we read in Engels' "Socialism Utopian and Scientific," "the thoughts within his brain were not the more or less abstract pictures of actual things and processes, but conversely things and their evolution were only the realized picture of the Idea existing somewhere from eternity, before the world was. This way of thinking turned everything upside down and completely reversed the actual connection of things in the world"[7] About the same time — this was in 1873 — Marx wrote in the Preface to the first volume of his Kapi-

[5] Engels, F., "Socialism, Utopian and Scientific," p. 95. A popular version in English dress of the same author's "Anti-Dühring."

[6] See especially Friedrich Feuerbach, "Die Religion der Zukunft."

[7] Engels, F., "Socialism, Utopian and Scientific," p. 86, and in "Anti-Dühring," p. 30.

tal: "To Hegel the life process of the human brain, i. e., the process of thinking which, under the name of the Idea he even transformed into an independent subject, is the demiurgos of the real world, and the world is only the external, phenomenal form of the Idea. With me, on the contrary, the ideal is nothing else than the material world reflected by the human mind, and translated into forms of thought."

The dialectic now became a simple affair. It was, as Engels observes in his "Anti-Dühring," "nothing but the science of the universal laws of motion and evolution in nature, human society, and thought." That is to say, Marx and Engels transferred the thought of relativity from the field of psychology, or better still of induction, to the field of historiography. It was clear to them that what Hegel treated only as a mode of individual reasoning was really a principle of progress by which past and future might be explained. If one judgment gives rise to an opposite the fusion of the two being a new truth, then surely historical epochs could similarly move by extremes. If contradiction was the leading characteristic of cognition, why not overlapping of ideas and conditions the core of history? If we have partial identity in a continuous flux of realities, why should not different historical epochs be linked by institutions only partly in harmony with them? The predetermination of conclusions by their premises surely had a counterpart in the casual connection between successive environments, their particulars and interlaced aspects.

§ 3. **The Marxian Statement of the Economic Interpretation of History.**— Thus the Logic of Hegel was converted by Marx and Engels into a temporal process governing the life of nations. What some have dubbed Economic Determinism is the outgrowth of Hegelian dialectics.[8] From the Enzyklopædie to " Das Kapital," this is a true line of descent! The Hegelian method, some have argued, was vigorously applied in Marx's analysis of exchange and surplus value. No doubt one may defend that view. But more direct is the relation between Hegelian metaphysics and the prosaic, empirical concept of history by which the indictment spread before us in Kapital is reduced to a mere detail.

The economic version of history develops rapidly in Marx's mind after Hegel and the Hegelian Left had challenged his attention. His intimate associations with the radicals in philosophy furthered greatly his intellectual progress. As early as 1843, à propos of a review of Hegel's Rechtsphilosophie, Marx says: " Theories among people are put into realization only so far as its practical needs demand. It isn't enough that ideas urge us to action; the actualities about us must generate the thoughts themselves before they may become practicable." [9] " We insist," adds Engels at a much later date, " that all hitherto formulated theories on ethics are the outgrowth, at last analysis, of the economic conditions ruling during the period in question." [10] Eighteenth century materialism was thus reapplied in a novel manner. The static view was displaced by the dynamic. Motion was given to a play of forces once pictured as at rest. Social facts are classified and compared as to their antecedents and stage of evolution relative to a given epoch. The economic interpretation is rounded out, and

[8] Compare the Marxian view with Feuerbach, L., in " Essence of Christianity " (translated by N. Evans), p. 23: " Time, and not the Hegelian dialectic, is the medium for uniting opposites in one and the same subject."

[9] Reprint in Mehring, F. Nachlass, Volume I.

[10] Engels, F., " Anti-Dühring."

by the time that Marx left the continent, to spend the remainder of his busy life on English soil, the materialistic conception of history is already full-blown. Modifications were later allowed by Engels,[11] doubtless as a sop to party demands, and also by way of defense against accusations hurled at his revered friend, but for all unbiased students the passage in Marx's " Critique of Political Economy " will rank as the most authoritative and most complete statement of scientific socialism.

We read in the Critique,[12] published many years before the first volume of Kapital came from the press: " In the social production which men carry on they enter into definite relations that are indispensable and independent of their will. These relations of production correspond to a definite stage of development of their material powers of production. The sum total of these relations of production constitutes the economic structure of society — the real foundation, on which legal and political superstructures arise, and to which correspond definite forms of social consciousness. The mode of production in material life determines the general character of the social, political, and spiritual processes of life. It is not the consciousness of men that determines their existence, but on the contrary their social existence determines their consciousness."

Let us note, before quoting further, that the material basis of life is said to consist of the means and modes of production, and that these give rise to " relations of production " which in turn furnish the substratum for all non-economic relations. Thus law and religion, art and

[11] Engels, F., "Der Spozialistische Akademiker," 1895 (Zwei Briefe).

[12] Marx, K., "Critique of Political Economy," Preface, 1859. English translation by N. I. Stone, published by Ch. Kerr & Co.

science receive their impress from the mold into which they are (according to Marx) *necessarily* cast.

But Marx goes on to show how economic relations are everchanging, the superstructure therefore becoming likewise unstable. Different rates of change are virtually referred to. A maladaptation of customs to conditions in the concrete is the result which is generally accompanied by social unrest. The Zeitgeist " must be explained from the contradictions in our collective living, from the existing conflict between the social forces of production and the relations of production." These latter are known to us as " the property relations " because of the stage of economic development that mankind has now arrived at. When the faultline in these strata of social life becomes too marked an upheaval may naturally be expected. Changes then will come rapidly. In the facts of the present moment we have the part determiners of a future crisis, a thought put by Marx as follows: " No social order ever disappears before all the productive forces, for which there is room in it, have been developed; and new, higher relations of production never appear before the material conditions of their existence have matured in the womb of the old society. Therefore mankind always takes up only such problems as it *can solve*, since, looking at the matter more closely, we will always find that the problem itself arises only when the material conditions necessary to its solution already exist, or at least are in the process of formation."

By this route then Marx has finally reached the point which relates most closely to his practical aims. He reminds us of the cosmic principle governing all life, and adds: " The bourgeois relations of production are the last antagonistic form of the social process of production — antagonistic not in the sense of individual antagonism, but antagonism arising from conditions surrounding the life of individuals in society. But at the same time the productive forces developing in the work of bourgeois society create the material conditions for the solution of that antagonism."

The economic analysis thus becomes simply a monumental proof of a theorem regarding historical evolution. Surplus theory and the socialization of capital are concepts centering about the Economic Interpretation of History. The misery of the masses, Marx demonstrates, is bound to end because beliefs and laws change with the material, economic environment. The case of the proletariat rests with the gods who laid down a mighty principle of life, but also with man to the extent that he is able to utilize the principle. Things move in a cycle, or perhaps we should say, in a spiral course leading upward. Capitalism is doomed, for it leads to exploitation of labor, to overproduction and unemployment, to vast combinations of capital destructive of small enterprise, and hence to rebellion on the part of an outraged populace.

The Marxian idea of history, for this reason, could not fail to buoy up the spirits of those who, resentful of their employers' tactics, yet saw no way of regenerating them by peaceful methods.

CHAPTER IV

THE ECONOMIC INTERPRETATION OF HISTORY (Continued)

§ 1. Importance of the Economic Interpretation of History.— A correct interpretation of history is important because of its bearing on our future conduct. Logically we should be guided by events of the past, for history is only a record of past events which resulted from the interaction of human nature and of environment. If as a result of certain actions a situation developed which, in reviewing it, we dislike we should feel prompted to do differently next time. This is the significance of all interpretations of the past, the Marxian not excluded.

Marx chose three points in his contemplation of history and made these his loadstar for speculations on the future. They were first, a division of events into the economic and non-economic, second, the establishment of a causal relation between the two, and third the explanation of misery as a maladjustment of past and present. Grant these features, and the paramount importance of his attempt must appear at once. History consists of records of past events, and these were once the present. The historian, then, treats of social processes as well as the sociologist or economist, only he studies them as something old and completed. The historian speaks of completed series of events; the student of contemporary events regards them as processes still under way.

A critique of the Marxian economic interpretation of history will turn on the points made by Marx himself, but it will also aim to restate, when necessary, those facts of the social process which relate to the Marxian program of reform. If socialism wishes to change the social order it must acquaint itself with the precise meaning of maladjustment, of causal relation, and of the economic interpretation of history in general. Only thus can it obtain elements for a theory of prosperity which it seeks to formulate; only thus can concepts of justice, democracy, and progress assume definiteness. The limits as well as the possibilities of socialism are given by the analysis of the social process which the Marxian interpretation of history involves.

Marx speaks of cause and effect. He held the economic data responsible for the character of the superstructure. There was no equivocation on that subject. He is very plain in his statements. But what is cause and correlation? If the economic and non-economic facts are related, of what sort is this correlation? And how do we find such interrelations? The Marxian theorem compels us to face these questions. It is a step in our general appreciation of the socialistic platform to ascertain the nature of cause and correlation. Correlation has to do with the grouping of events that fill our life. Cause has to do with classifying the events for future use. The study of cause and effect turns on a selection of elements in a situation with a view to forecasting future correlations or to controlling them, if we dare and care.

§ 2. **The Problem of Correlation.**— All our experience is of events happening in groups. We do not sense things as units entirely segregated from other units any more than we see individuals living as hermits, secluded from the rest of the world. Events come in series, in succession or in coexistence. We see lightning and hear thunder. We look out into the street and behold innumerable facts related in various ways: the children playing by groups, the traffic in a certain order, the array of houses and the framing of it all in an environment of sky and nature and conditions of the weather, in space and in time. Everything thus appears to us as happening either simultaneously or successively. In the former case, as when I see a tree with its trunk and foliage, its color and size, or the shape of its leaves, the logician speaks of coexistence of facts. In the latter case, when for instance the clouds gather before a storm, the streets next begin to be pelted with big drops of rain, and eventually a gust blows amid flashes from the sky, the logician speaks of sequences. The events happen in a certain order in time.

The problem of correlation, which leads up to the question of causation, consists of two parts. The first is the facts of *remembrance* of correlations, and the second is the method of *discovering* new correlations which are not obvious to the sense. The picture I get of the street is one presented immediately to my eye. The correlations are discovered by being seen. That is all. We learn in this manner to adjust ourselves to the facts present. But without memory the adjustment would be incomplete, since instinctive reactions do not always answer. The difference between animal and man is largely the difference in memory, though of course animals also remember things.

Our ability to remember is grounded in the facts of metabolism and of a nervous mechanism which have been disclosed chiefly during the nineteenth century. For the psychologist the fundamental facts in consciousness are sensation, selection, and memory. We have the principle of sensing things, of being stimulated and responding, of responding not to all stimuli, but only to some, and of storing impressions so they may color future impressions.

This trio of principles forms the foundation on which most facts of consciousness and behavior rest. But for the purposes in hand it is more convenient to take sensation for granted, and to single out for special mention the nature of association, before trying to understand cause and effect.

We are stimulated from the outside, that is peripherally, or from within, that is centrally. Anything calculated to produce physico-chemical changes, no matter how minute, in our body, represents a stimulus. We live in the midst of such excitations, and we respond to them often. One stimulus may produce several distinct reactions, or one reaction may be the result of several stimuli. This follows from the interlacing of the carriers of excitation.

The human body, in one aspect, is a vast network of nerves, and the nervous mechanism is a system of conduction units by which stimuli are converted into more or less complex responses. The unit is the neurone of which billions exist, and over which stimuli are transmitted to reach the proper centers and connections that ensure suitable reaction. The end of life is action; the purpose of the neurone is the conduction of stimuli for right reaction. In a reflex action the stimulus is carried over a simple arc connecting receptor with motor organ. The twitch of a muscle is a case in hand. But the great majority of reactions are established more circuitously, by means of switchings of excitation, of redirection in the spine and in the cortex, so that highly elaborated series of movements, of ideas and feelings become possible.

And this is particularly made possible by the capacity of the organism to remember. Man remembers experiences. His nervous mechanism is said to respond in the sense that it carries stimuli, and carries them the more readily the oftener they come, though other principles also decide. Physiologically the explanation is a lessening of resistance to the current that travels over the neurones. It is inconsequential whether we imagine the transmission as one akin to the burning of a fuse leading to discharge and detonation, or whether the transmission partakes of the nature of an electric current. But it is important to note the effect of repetition upon the nerve cells. The places at which the neurones connect — the synapses — yield more readily to a second or third than to a first excitation, other things being equal. It is like folding a garment. Gradually a crease is made, and subsequent folding is easy; it follows the old crease. Thus paths are made from continual walking in the same line. Thus rivers dig their channel through solid rock. And similarly the excitation of the optical nerve survives the stimulus itself. After-images are somewhat like memory. The effect outlasts the cause.

We learn by remembering, that is by reducing the resistance originally offered to stimuli and to their passages. Either we are naturally predisposed toward the acceptance of a stimulus, or we *acquire* the ability to receive and transmit it. "Learning," in the words of a psychologist, "is a process of making easier the passage of an impulse from neurone to neurone." [1] The function of education is to control the stimuli reaching us, at the beginning of life, from the outside, and later from within also. It is to cull out the bad, to strengthen the desirable, and to redirect them so as to effectuate the best possible adjustments, that we receive instruction.

The outward proof of memorizing, of lessening the resistance to impulses and their transmission, is the forming

[1] Pillsbury, W. B., "Essentials of Psychology." Revised Edition, p. 55.

of habits. Habituation is one of the most fruitful of all capacities. It is the most common of traits. We all become addicted to things; we all learn to react habitually. We learn, in short, to do things without paying attention, without noticeable effort, without being conscious of the act of doing. Thus with walking, eating, dressing, playing an instrument, etc., etc. Habituation means a sense of comfort because of the ease with which things are done and reacted to. It is not merely a question of motor reactions, however; a response in belief and ideals is equally in point. What we are used to we commonly like and prefer to strange things. The strange is usually distasteful to us, unless some features in it, reminding us of features in familiar things, break down our instinctive or acquired aversion.

The effect of frequent repetition is therefore an attitude of expectancy. We are keyed up to anticipate events, and to react suitably. Experience permits us thus to save time and energy. Habituation means looking forward to events because they happened in the past. If they suddenly cease to happen, we feel disappointed or queer. Nothing jars like habits broken off at short notice, like regularities ending of a sudden. The converse to this jarring of unforeseen interruption upon our nerves, upon our consciousness, is our disposition to believe the familiar things, and to believe that they will occur again. So many successions of day and night, for instance, have occurred in our individual lives, that the non-recurrence is thought impossible. It is only when other experiences directly, or by a process of reasoning soon to be discussed, induce us to consider the possibility of a non-recurrence that we fail to believe in its necessity. Thus with the repeated appearance of a certain number in the throw of the dice. Here contrary experiences tend to weaken our attitude of expectation. But in general repetition means anticipation, or as the logician has put it: We infer things by way of enumeration. We number events and then cherish beliefs accordingly. If winter has always, or so many times, brought snow and ice, we expect more ice and snow the next winter. We learn to induce future occurrences from the past.

This is the first important circumstance in a study of our inference and correlation. The second is selection and attention.

Not all things are noticed and remembered. Our environment consists really only of the facts we react upon. We sense things according to definite principles and ignore more or less fully everything else. Or we see things, but do not pay particular attention to them, that is we do not make them the center of things, we do not focus our mental eye upon them to the exclusion of much else. Only for particular purposes do we single out events for prolonged study. Only because the reaction to stimuli serves to protect and develop our interests do we select our stimuli. Selection is a necessary corollary to specialization of means and ends in species, each specie having its own characteristics of needs and habits.

Our selection of possible stimuli is governed by objective and subjective conditions. The intensity of the stimulus is an example of the first kind; the facts of training, of the second. According to our general schooling and experience, according to purposes at the moment when the stimulus is present, according to immediately preceding sensations, to predispositions inherited, or to pressure brought to bear upon us by our fellowmen, we notice or ignore things, treat them indifferently or make them the special subject of our investigation. We shut out most elements in a given situation from our vision. This is true not only in an optical sense, but likewise of our method of learning.

From the general law of selection follows our habit of comparing things. Our system becomes attuned to similar stimuli in different ensembles of facts, or to different stimuli in like ensemble of facts. It is essential to the maintenance of life to discriminate and to compare. From infancy on we classify stimuli and develop our responses specifically. Classification may not be conspicuously carried on; no more than motor reactions always depend on concentration of effort. But comparison and grouping of data are daily practices without which the environment could not be mastered. We remember to select and compare, and we also select our stimuli in order to learn the right reactions.

But note that as a result of this eternal process of attention a *group of events never really embraces all* of the factors in the group. In a thunder storm, e. g., I see many things, but not nearly all. I select only as my instincts command, or as experiences seem to justify. Innumerable elements in the situation called a thunderstorm remain unobserved by me. I may at a later date see more of them, or I may have reasons for looking for more. Or I may have seen a greater number at an earlier date, but forgotten. All this varies and depends on the principles of selection and remembering already referred to. In this survey the only notable fact is the variable number of facts constituting a complete situation — what we call the correlation regularly recurring, such as the aforesaid thunderstorm. We seem to have the complete situation, but do not, as later experiences may prove. For practical ends at a given moment the correlation may be perfect, but it does not remain so. Our perception, in short, is of selected materials in a structure. We perceive salient features, what to us seems essential according to particular, perhaps practical, ends, but this subjective picture may not correspond to reality, or what at another time seems reality. Percepts are always abstractions.

But before fully understanding the percept the principle of association must be invoked. It is through associations that we greatly enrich our power of reactions and facilitate our search for new truths.

The theory of association may be stated as the belief everywhere held, and by science duly recognized as a fact, that our ideas are governed by the past. Connections of the past govern the reproduction of ideas. To have perceived means not only to recognize by force of memory, but also to see anew in the light of experiences not perhaps directly connected with the prototype of the particular new experience. If for instance I have seen the striking of a match to lead to ignition I may remember this, and the motions involved in the act of striking will become the easier the oftener I repeat the performance. This is simply a case of memory. But the effect of association is the recall of events *not* happening at the time of recall. To see a match struck, for instance, and to recall the sound it usually makes, without hearing it at the time, that is memorizing by association.

The physiological aspect of this important fact lies in the intertwining of nerve paths, and in the existence of association areas in the cortex, whose function is primarily the connecting of different sensations, or of movements with sensations for adjustment to the largest possible number of stimuli. To quote from an authority: "When a group of neurones was active at the time of the original experience, paths of connection were formed, synapses were opened between them, and later, when any element of the complex is aroused in any way, the impulse tends to spread over the partially open synapses to the other elements of the whole."[2] That is to say, we may imagine different nerve paths to have part of their course in common. They converge and part again. Excitations from different sources travel partly over the same path, and at the points of contiguity of the neurones they are connected so that one stimulus may arouse others, and lead to a long series of reactions. The stimuli may be aroused peripherally or centrally. Ideas are for the purpose of the psychologist as truly sensations as those generated by outside facts.

The principles of association are those first suggested by the Greeks, namely of association by resemblance, contrast, contiguity or continuity. But evidently this is a mere classification, not an explanation of the process. Nor are the four truly distinct, since resemblance and contrast imply comparisons in space and time, which probably account for all rearousals. And again, as our writer admits, the association is more truly one of neurones than of ideas, the association not following strictly the principles laid down by the ancients. Thus "not only must we limit the application of the doctrine of associations by the assertion that it is the neurones at the basis of the elements of ideas that are associated rather than the ideas themselves, but we must also recognize that associations give only the possibility of recall, and that *selection* must be made between the possibilities by more remote factors."[3] We do not associate all things seen together in space or time. Inhibitions come naturally, and are specially cultivated by education. Thus attention becomes

[2] Pillsbury, W. B., "Fundamentals of Psychology," p. 223.
[3] *Ibidem*, p. 227.

fruitful, and adjustment rapid and exact. In other words, the selective forces affect association as well as memory itself.

Yet the fundamental fact is as stated. We are again and again led to recall the past by stimuli in the present somehow related to stimuli in an earlier situation. The principle reminds one of the Lamarckian contention according to which acquired traits are inherited. The son, it is said, will act somewhat as the environment made the father act, even though the son lives in a different environment. It is again a case of memory and habituation, but this time by indirect stimulation. Recall in this manner enlarges our capacity for learning. "Learning," we are told, "is always the formation of connections between neurones; retention is always the persistence of the connection, or the partial openness of synapses which permits an impression to pass from one to the other of the connected elements: recall is the rearousal of the whole complex by some one of the elements that may be stimulated from the outside world, directly or indirectly."[4] A part suffices to arouse the whole; that is the main characteristic of association.

A distinction should, however, be made between recall of events regularly correlated, and a recall of events which only in part recur regularly. If, to return to the illustration of the match, I expect ignition at the striking of a match because it has always resulted in ignition, this is direct association of events invariably coupled. They belong together as integral parts of a series, and have so been classified. But if, on hearing a melody, I am reminded of childhood scenes, and then perhaps of a long chain of happenings covering many years, relating to places and persons nowhere before me now while I hear

[4] *Ibidem*, p. 223.

the melody, then the association is indirect, of things not regularly recurring or correlated. The only binding link is perchance a single quality of tone, or a mistake made in playing the instrument, or a peculiar way of ending the performance, and so on. A few elements are sufficient to reconstruct all the elements, or at least a great many elements, in the older situation. The *one* thing held in common by the old and the new series of events is responsible for the recall of all the rest in the old series. Thus ideas skip and travel at an amazing rate. Thus in the twinkle of an eye one may traverse the universe and rehearse a lifetime of struggles. Indirect association is the important principle for the extension of our knowledge, and for the understanding of trifles in our daily conduct. It is the *transfer* of ideas that counts, more than the recollection of events experienced together regularly. Or, to put it differently, the association by resemblance (or contrast) is far more important than association by contiguity and succession. The latter helps to explain *expectation and beliefs*, but the former is instrumental in *multiplying* the data for belief.

Just what elements in the new sensations guide my concatenation of thoughts, and in what direction it ultimately leads me, depends, as already remarked, to some extent upon the general laws of selection. I am sure to be influenced by previous associations, by moods of the moment, by ideas uppermost in my mind, by facts of temperament and of training. They all determine the scope and nature of my transfer of ideas, they all influence us in our search for new facts.

The principles of finding a new correlation connect with this circumstance. If the correlation is not one directly submitted to my senses, such as the sequence of work and fatigue, or the coexistence of flame and heat, special efforts must be made to find it. This is our task from birth to death. We continually look for new groups of events, see them repeat themselves, and add one correlation to the next by virtue of memory and selection.

One way of ascertaining new correlations is to try out alternatives. If, for instance, I cannot open a door which I have opened often and expect to be able to open by the usual method, I will be puzzled for a while and then look for the cause. That is, since just now we are not interested in cause per se — I will try to get the complete set of facts connected with the impossibility of opening the door. I may try to lift it by the knob, or press it downward or push it toward me or from me, or shake it, or look for obstructions on either side if I can do so. I go on the supposition that many elements go into the situation which is new to me, and that I may hit upon some elements essential to its not opening, just as I had known some elements to be essential to its opening. I may come upon the factors and remember them.

Or suppose I have a watch which keeps good time in one place, but loses time in another. If I feel so inclined I may ascertain the pertinent facts at random. Let us assume, at any rate, that I am guided by no prior experience of any kind, an abstraction permissible for the purpose. I then might use my developed powers of selection and attention. I begin to compare two different situations and to classify events according to resemblance and difference. I say, here is my habit of wearing the watch, the way it lies in my pocket, the way and time in and at which I wind it up, the facts about the watch itself, my way of walking and using it when consulting the dial. And so on. I may enumerate and put in two columns the facts I hold alike and those peculiar to each situation. It is likely that I find many similarities and some differences.

The whole procedure so far is that made famous by Mill's canons of induction. I compare and tabulate results. Mill pointed out that where all things except one are held in common by two or more different situations the one differential assumes unusual significance. But let us note simply that at last I have found some differences which I think sufficient to round out the new situation in which the watch does not keep time. I may now take the watch several times from one place to the other and note that each time in place A it runs accurately, and in place B it falls behind. If I repeat this often enough, what will be the effect on my opinion about the watch? I shall simply come to believe that in the future also the watch will fail me in one situation, but respond well in the other. The force of repetition will set in as usual. On the principle of induction by enumeration I shall develop a belief that past correlations will recur. I shall speak of a law, for the watch, of keeping time and losing time respectively in two different places. Laws are nothing but such regular recurrences of sequences and coexistences, as logicians found out centuries ago.

Very well. But it is not likely that I shall experiment in that fashion. Scientists particularly do not ascertain new correlations, that elude the five senses, in such a haphazard manner. They proceed with some eye to economy. They select the facts to be watched, and shape beforehand their plans. How, then, are thinkers as a rule guided? What is the modus operandi in reasoning? What is the approved and common method of inference?

It is *reasoning by analogy*. It is by resort to memory and association. Instead of dwelling long on deduction and canons of induction Mill, as modern psychology sees it, might have better put analogies in the foreground of his discussion. Inference by analogy is the rule rather than the exception. And not only that, it also marks the nature and limits of most of our knowledge.

In the case of my watch, then, I shall do as I did when trying to open the door. I shall proceed by hypothecation in accord with the dictates of association and memory. I tried to open the door by lifting or downward pressing at the knob, because I knew that wood swelled, and that this might make the opening difficult. Only after these expedients failed would I normally look for other faults, or for some one on the other side holding the door, or for its being locked contrary to orders.

As to the watch, I cast about for explanations also. That is, I cast about for groups of events which in their entirety would give the experienced result. I am influenced by the principle of association. I look for a factor which other situations share with the new one. Or rather, one or more elements in the new situation remind me of other situations containing many more than the particular factors. I am led to make comparison in a certain direction. Guided by knowledge, we say. Yes, guided by knowledge, or by a fund of associations, which is much the same thing. Instead of finding the differentials therefore by piecemeal classification and enumeration I resort to a circuitous method. I do in reasoning what the enterpriser does when he substitutes machinery for manual work. I take indirect routes which at first have cost much effort and time, but by their aid I can now achieve results more expeditiously.

I am willing to look for differences and resemblances by comparing a former situation with the present, because in the past such *partial resemblances have meant resemblance in toto.* Association directs me; but it does not affect us all equally. Association leads to observation of likenesses and unlikenesses. A few of them are quickly noted and kept in mind. And now I fall back again on the principle of enumeration. Since up to date situations have proven alike in all parts when only some of them were formerly observed to be alike, and since I have witnessed long chains of happenings to recur exactly *as I predicted* after having found some of the happenings similar to some noticed at other times, I infer a like aggregate result for similar future chains of happenings. And furthermore, the fact that part resemblances often mean complete resemblance, and that a recurrence of a former entire series is the *likelier the more nearly* its beginning events resemble those of an older correlation, also induces me to compare the nature of the resemblance.

But my faith is reënforced from still another quarter. Namely, it is a common observation that the distribution of events is either regular or irregular. If regular I attribute it to a law of nature which comprises the regularities just discussed — correlations which form the bulk of scientific knowledge. Or I attribute it to human interference and design. Man always places himself in the middle of a situation. He feels himself to be the planner and architect of his fortunes. When he acts, the results of regularity are of his making and hence, he avers, explained. But when neither a natural law nor the hand of man can be predicated as part of the regularity of events their distribution is felt to be a chance event. An irregularity is expected. We see irregularity where we do not refer one group of facts to *another group*, just as we ascribe to chance what is really an unknown principle about which perhaps we care nothing.

Probability then is a forecast based on retrospects. The chance of regularity is the greater the more definite our comprehension of laws or of human design back of it. And my belief that a whole series of events will recur when some of them have in the past proven to be part of a particular larger series, is the stronger the greater the number of events common to both situations. The more resemblances pile up, and the oftener they recur, the more convinced I am that the entire series is of the old sort; and I am willing to predict accordingly. This is the reason for my inferring things by analogy. In this manner I am led to discover the new correlation centering about my watch when it loses time. Thuswise the principles of association, selection, and memory collaborate to help me discover new truths.

Reasoning by analogy indeed becomes so habitual that often we are unaware of using it. Thus recognition of things may be regarded as much as an act of inference as of mere perception. A physician, for instance, may not diagnose a case by exhaustive, systematic enumeration of symptoms as observed in the study of my watch. Association may be direct and suggest at once the nature of the disease. He sees certain events or characteristics, is reminded of similar ones connecting with a malady called scarlet fever, and at once pronounces the new case to be one of scarlet fever. The tendency to recognize things as alike is always strong, when some one element of similarity exists. And the fact that a disease is in question strengthens the inclination to infer from analogy. But of course, this first recognition may soon be superseded by cautious study. If contradictory evidence presents itself new lines of associations and of reasoning will be opened.

If I see some objects on a table, looking round and reddish, of a certain texture and size or shape, I will immediately call them apples, and all of them apples, without having compared them carefully with another object known to be an apple, or even without rehearsing my own experiences with like objects. Recognition, that is "the reference of an event or object to some earlier time and place,"[5] satisfies the needs of the case. Thus also, if a boy should be run over by a vehicle, or somebody fall down the stairway and appear to be seriously injured. I have seen no details, but infer so quickly by association that the recognition is almost a single act. I believe the entire situation to be such and such because part of it resembles an earlier one of a certain kind. In brief, my perception is a *partial summary* of events which are rearoused by new events.

The percept is a compound much as water is one. The joint result of individual actions is no mere summation, but a new product. Perception is more than association if that is to mean a stringing together of sensations, as we might thread pearls. The Herbartian doctrine of apperception was a great step in advance precisely because it realized this characteristic of perception and freed us from the older mechanistic notion.

"Percepts," according to one psychologist, "are selected groups of sensations in which images are incorporated as an integral part of the whole process."[6] In the words of another competent authority, quoted several times before, "the world that we have in memory or in reason is not the sum of particular experiences; it is always the mass of particular experiences worked over, and crystallized about standards."[7] "What is perceived is not merely a mass of sensations nor is it a single sensation that suggests some other single sensation or group of sensations; rather is it a type, an organized product of many

[5] *Ibidem,* p. 366.

[6] Titchener, E. B., "Textbook of Psychology," p. 367.

[7] Pillsbury, W. B., "Psychology of Reasoning," p. 76.

experiences which have finally given rise to a construct consistent with all of our different related experiences." [8] The percept, then, is the result of many correlations not having all events in common, but many of them. Percepts are averages, so to say. Roughly speaking they describe situations, but each new situation will have its own peculiarities, and each new act of sensing will reckon with the differences.

I perceive what is important, and I sense what is conspicuous. A picture is an abstract for that reason. It has meaning because I see only part of the lines and planes in it, and not all, and because I see them in certain relations of space to each other. My perspective is spoiled when I step too close. The picture goes and a tangle of lines and dots is left, but it conveys no idea. It only irritates me. Thus everything perceived is a cluster of elements many of which recur over and over again, in approximately the same juxtaposition of time and space. But the fact that percepts are only approximations is of great importance to our analysis of correlation and cause, for by virtue of it science becomes fallible and plastic, subject to correlation and growth, an estimate rather than a set of laws immutable for all times.

It is not necessary to preach phenomenalism in order to agree to the relativity of scientific truths. Nor will all assent to William James' dictum that pragmatists are necessarily realists. The core of the epistemological problem is the fact of reasoning, which is based on data of psychology. The Beyond need not detain us, especially since all philosophies of the absolute have broken down by assuming part of what they sought to demonstrate independently.

[8] Pillsbury, W. B., "Fundamentals of Psychology," pp. 395–96. See also the same writer's "Psychology of Reasoning," pp. 90 & 97.

But there is no doubt that inference by analogy accounts for most of our beliefs and of our knowledge even such as is verified in an objective sense. The thought of chance distribution and of probability is doubtless a product of such reasoning. The explanation here offered of the method for discovering new correlations is itself an instance of inference from analogy. And mathematics and history are almost entirely limited to such procedure, the latter admitting it frankly, while the latter was long held to work with instruments infallible and inscrutable. Historians reason by reference to occurrences in their own environment, or by deductions from human nature, that is by analogy. The great bulk of verities that the social student and ethicists of the old type gave to the world were unprovable. They were true in so far as they accorded with the principles of thinking just mentioned. Put otherwise: They were and always will be true in so far as *modes of thinking among men are the same*, due to millions of years of environments shared in common by our ancestors. Evolution has made us in some things alike, and our reasoning process is part of this universal human nature, though *our funds of knowledge and of associations, and hence the trend and power of our reasoning* vary enormously. Sociological events are scattered in time and place. Besides, they are non-reproducible in their entirety. We express this by admitting that an indeterminate number of factors enter into a given situation, whose control is ordinarily beyond us. In this sense most sociological events cannot be "proven." Yet we can measure by averages and rejoice in the recurrence of averages — approximately and for limited period of time or areas or groups of people. Insurance rates thus become possible, though rates will change with conditions. Mortality figures thus assume much definiteness. and are deemed reliable, though they change in time and place. Averages, for that matter, prevail everywhere, both in natural and social science.

Is there no proof, then? Or better: What is proof? When is something absolutely true? The question is natural because deduction is supposed to furnish irrefutable proofs such as should satisfy the most ambitious of metaphysicians.

We may answer yes or no according to the nature of facts in question, and according to our notion of truth. Proof namely is in the eating of the pudding, which means that all so-called verification ("making true") is by appeal to the senses. But in as much as the senses differ we cannot believe that all things are true in *exactly* the same way to all people. We can only say that *some* elements in a situation will be perceived by all in like manner, and that this rough correspondence is equivalent to proof. A proposition is proven when demonstrated to the eye or ear or taste, etc. It is proven true when it "works well," when the application of science, e. g., brings desired results. This does not mean that truth depends on application, or science on commercialization. No, it means simply that some judgments are true to all in so far as our sensing or perceptions *veer about types common to us all.*

But where objective verification is impossible, as in the case with most of the verdicts of social science, there belief of *experts* is tantamount to proof. The general run of people will accept expert advice as truth because they are swayed naturally by superiority or by the socialized agents of control. And if both verification and expertness are lacking, then the opinion of the *majority* becomes the standard. Mere number wins in many cases. For want of better evidence we go to the multitude. Thus public opinion becomes truth, and thus our ideals seem to us indisputable truths. We have arrived at them by much the same methods of reasoning that the scientist uses. The ways of common sense are the ways of science.

The chief difference between the layman and the scientist is therefore not one of methods, but one of instruments and results. Science has inestimable advantages in control, measurement, and associations. It may isolate phenomena, select its facts carefully and place them in surroundings that make observation of details possible and easy. It uses artificial means of reproducing events so as to be able to know exactly what is going on. This power of rehearsing the course of events in a given correlation leads to the establishment of new correlations by elimination and introduction of factors chosen for special purposes. A plan of action characterizes the investigations of the professional which the tyro rarely knows of.

And besides, there are means of measurement vastly superior to the ordinary. An indirect method is here the chief advantage. Differences in weight and length, in force and volume that could not be detected by the naked eye become marked as soon as special devices are called into service. The micrometer and the seismograph, the stop-watch and galvanometer, or the vacuum-balance are invaluable aids in minute differentiations that may lead to a new conception of the situation studied.

The fund of associations grows steadily; partly because records are filed for future reference so that the memory of science is made more reliable than that of the average individual, and partly because incessant specialized study enlarges the fund of known facts that will serve to stimulate further inference. From the known to the unknown is always the course in learning, but it has special significance for the trained investigator who deliberately sets himself problems remote from everyday experiences. A large fund of associations is indispensable in his undertaking. The greater the number of correlations, the larger is the choice of resemblances and differences, and consequently the less liable to error the reasoning from analogy. Verification may or may not be definitive, but the subsumption of a new particular under an old generality is facilitated by the increase of facts as such.

People frequently are called illogical when they are only ignorant. They are incapable of reasoning on a certain subject because their fund of associations is too small. They may do better somewhere else. They may also lack the kind of memory type that aids in specialized pursuits of knowledge. It is well known that not all are equally adepts in the same field. We differ, but need not be dunces because we fail in one direction. According to our powers of visualization our associations may promote inventiveness or stifle it. Some are the prey of their associations which make them roam aimlessly without focusing on a point. Others gain by their memory and cultivate a habit of thought, of fruitful thinking. This is really possible, though not often practiced.

Sciences also grow. Sciences shift their boundary lines and the centers of emphasis which from period to period characterize their inquiries. They start out with well defined lines for subject matter and scope, but eventually feel less sure about the divisions. Chemistry and physics thus have points in common, where workers meet and find problems overlapping. Biology is no longer considered to be worlds apart from psychology, and the social sciences have always been at odds over the precise demarcation of their borders.

The correlations grow, and the factors in each correlation increase. The tendency is commonly toward further reduction of apparent irreducibles. We are driven from one ultimate to another. We divide more minutely and distinguish things by finer lines. Physics for instance adds the corpuscle to the atom and makes gravity a function of motion. Chemistry no longer reckons with atoms and molecules merely. It recognizes in addition isomerism, and wonders about the relation of the elements, the transmutation of matter being an observed fact. New elements in a narrow sense, and new constituents of a correlation in a wider sense have crept into the chemist's range of vision.

What was once held to be the make-up of a good soil now seems like an inadequate analysis. We consider much more than the ratio in which chemical elements are combined, and the ratio in which such compounds appear in the soil. We figure on many other things before pronouncing on the worth of it. Similarly the biologist has gone from one reduction to another. The cell has ceased to be a homogeneous unit. We now regard it as a highly elaborate mechanism for bodily functions or for reproduction. We have gone from plasm to nucleus, and from nucleus to, say, chromatin, and from that to chromosomes, and thence to determinants in the chromosomes which we think are the bearers of heredity. An indeterminate number of factors is said to be lodged in the chromosomes, the combination and placements of which vary, and lead to varying results in the individual. Psychology no longer speaks of "faculties," as if they were entities functioning in separate compartments. Consciousness is too complex a thing for that. The percept is recognized as a joint effect of innumerable sensations present directly or by recall. It is like a mosaic that for all its variegation and numberless bits presents a unified whole, an agreeable picture and a plan adaptable to definite ends.

And so with most sciences. The substitution by the economist of the law of the proportionality of factors for the Ricardian notion of diminishing returns is a further instance of growth in factors and correlations. There is no need for expatiating on a familiar fact. Everywhere the sense of simplicity in correlations is lost. We see a greater number of elements, a larger number of variables whose measurement becomes increasingly difficult. The impression of preciseness and absolute regularity is lost in proportion as we see and know more. Science is not as cocksure and dogmatic as it used to be. "The progress of science," as one philosopher puts it, "is a process of successive approximations, in which new and more precise, more probable and more extended inductions result from partially verified deductions, and from those contradictions that correct the implicit hypotheses." [9]

That is the true state of affairs. Science approximates and revises. It must periodically face discrepancies and contradictions. Doubt alternates with belief. Doubt is a feeling resulting from a conflict of ideas, of associations. Any one who has tried to solve a problem in the abstract, or to overcome an unexpected practical obstacle, knows what misery accompanies a clash of trains of reasoning, each good in itself, but in discord with others. When such memory associations come to blows, as it were, the mind suffers as a whole. It means misery and sleepless nights, perhaps loss of appetite and incapacity for routine actions. Doubt is the opposite of belief which is the fruit of habituations developed at leisure.

Science, then, has limitations which bear on all matters of study and are of significance even for the socialist who

[9] Enriques, F., "Problems of Science," p. 166.

would reform the world. Science is not the simple device for ascertaining irrefutable truths that socialism has often pictured it to be. It is a case of change in venue. Laws are mutable, though of many things we all obtain like impressions. Mill's canons erred in promising science more than it has accomplished. In particular is the Canon of Difference no more infallible than any of the others, for the missing link or cause may be much more than a single agent. Its reduction may be impending.

What we are sure of, so far as modern psychological evidence is concerned, is the existence of *one method of reasoning* employed by all sciences. The number of sciences may be increased indefinitely according to our conception of correlations of events, but they all resort to the same mode of discovery and of generalization. Deduction and induction, for the same reason, are not two distinct methods, but two aspects of one single process of reasoning. In the syllogism the conclusion follows from the premises because we have always known a part of a thing to be smaller than the whole. This axiom decides in the end. But the rules of distribution result from the principles of association that are used in collocating two premises so as to make their bearing upon the conclusion plain. Induction underlies the construction of the syllogism, though *after* the premises are laid down a purely deductive act takes place. But it remains true, as was stated over a century ago, that the syllogism in itself cannot extend knowledge, because it assumes what at the moment is not verified or perhaps cannot be verified.

§ 3. **The Meaning of Causation.**— These things being so the meaning of cause and effect also becomes clear. In the words of J. S. Mill: Cause is "The sum total of conditions, positive and negative, taken together; the whole of the contingencies of every description, which being realized the consequent invariably follows."[10] And to quote from two later writers: "There is no particular difference between knowledge of causes, and our general knowledge of the combinations, or succession of combinations, in which the phenomena of nature are presented to us, or found to occur in experimental inquiry."[11] "Things are not either independent, or causative. All classes of phenomena are linked together, and the problem in each case is how close is the degree of association."[12]

That is to say, every factor in a given situation — no matter how far we may go in our choice of factors, is either cause *or* effect according to viewpoint and need. Objectively they function in this respect all in the same way, but our subjective choice leads to the designation of some *particular* facts as causes. All sequences and coexistences consist necessarily of causal relations, no matter how obscure. Even the random arrangement of furniture in a room represents cause and effect if one wishes to speak accurately. Any set of facts *is* cause and effect, of which some facts become causes in a narrow sense.

We select particulars on the principle of attention already discussed. Stimuli interest us in different ways. We react not in like ways to things. Our life is a process of adjustmet to physical and economic environment, such that some elements in a situation will seem vital while others are negligible. Causation is a selective act. To ascribe cause to something is to give it a special value for particular purposes. For instance, to say that cold freezes water into ice is a way of calling attention to a

[10] Mill, J. S., "Logic," Book III, Chapter 5, No. 3. Similarly also Venn, J., in his "Empirical Logic," p. 67.

[11] Jevons, W. S., "Principles of Science," Book II, Chapter 1.

[12] Pearson, K., "Grammar of Science," Edit. 1911, Volume 1, p. 166. See also p. 177.

factor influencing our behavior at the time. Many things go into the situation: The location of water, the atmospheric conditions, the qualities of matter in general and of water in particular, such as expansion, weight, translucency, etc., etc. But one group in the ensemble known as cold gets the credit or blame for the entire complex. Except by reference to will and will-to-live our designation of cause and effect must appear quite arbitrary.

Nietzsche, the German prophet of a revaluation of values, remarks in his "Will to Power" that "the so-called instinct of causality is nothing more than the fear of the unfamiliar, and the attempt at finding something in it which is already known."[13] That is a pithy way of stating one of the principles governing our designation of cause. We see ourselves as agents and call the facts about us frequently the effects of our action, we being the cause. The Ego is a unit. Its expressions are results of a will. We are cause and bring about effects. And just as people from time immemorial have personalized unexplained facts, making out of them gods in human shape or powers of human capacity magnified many times, so by reasoning from analogy we attribute a causative function to other live or moving factors in a situation. Fear prompts us, and introspection guides us in this step. Animals are pictured as agents, and inanimate things become causes when made conspicuous in some way.

A second principle in our choice of cause, then, is motion. In the midst of immobile things the moving appear more commonly as cause, if no other principle interferes. The falling of a leaf from a tree, for instance, is said to result from a gust of wind. The wind was felt or heard. The rotting of the stem of the leaf, the extra weight of it due to an excrescence on the underside, the condition of

[13] "The Will to Power, Aphorism," No. 551.

the twig whence it came, the law of gravitation — these and more facts were overlooked or taken for granted. The idea of force impelled us to hold the breeze responsible. Again. We say motion causes friction, not friction motion. This seems reasonable; but why? The two form a coexistence. We cannot set the moment at which friction ensues after motion has commenced. The two coincide absolutely. But motion is more apparent than friction, and back of motion is noticed, or understood to act, an agent who really is the causative fact we allude to.

Often, however, and in the third place, we distinguish between things controllable by man and those not so controllable. The former are then the causes, and the latter the effects, or the subliminal facts of no consequence. What cannot be changed we do not attack in a plan of action. We divide the world — say for purposes of reform — into variables and constants, thinking of the latter as facts unalterable. Thus the law of gravitation is taken for granted. We expect men to protect themselves against it in certain situations. We provide means of support for objects. Buildings and chairs are devices for utilizing or offsetting the general law. We do not blame the law when something falls. We ask people to be more careful and hold on to things, or to build better foundations.

Or suppose a man is found destitute of the means of livelihood. We can assign this to a hundred facts, but probably will not think of the man's stupidity first. Or, if we do, we proceed to emphasize another fact as cause. The pauper himself may complain of unemployment or illness in the family, or of an accident, and what not. Or we find him indolent, inattentive, intemperate, etc. Or we speak of hard times, of bad politics, of unfavorable weather for the sort of work the poor man wanted. The factors we can control or believe we can change become cause; the rest is ignored.

In the fourth place special purposes may guide us.[14] We speak of prejudices and axes to grind, of malice and ulterior motives, and like things that color our judgment and decide our choice of cause. Or it is the event nearest in time or place that looms up as cause, as when a crowd gathers in a street and I notice a boy looking for a coin. I make him the starting point of my location of cause and effect because I saw him and watched the number of onlookers grow after his loss. I do not ask why he dropped the coin, whether he was day-dreaming or had a nervous fit, or what led to day-dreaming. And so on. The nearest concrete and active factor becomes the cause. The murderer is arraigned and condemned partly for this reason. We either disdain searching into his history or that of the victim, in order to extend the chain of factors, or we take refuge in a postulate of freewill and then pronounce judgment.

We cannot trace all the intervening links in a lengthy chain of facts constituting a correlation regularly recurring. When a cow gives birth to a calf we ascribe the flow of milk to that event. We do not go back to the facts of fertilization that would logically form a more correct starting point for the whole correlation. Or say a war breaks out. Will not the cause be the occasion that historians distinguish from the "underlying" causes? And are not the remote "causes" certain facts preceding the declaration of war? Is it not plain that only a few

14 What is known as the pragmatic movement in philosophy has developed this point into a system of thought, of which Schiller, F. C. S., is a typical representative. See this writer's "Formal Logic," pp. 277 & 283. Likewise: Enriques, F., "Problems of Science," p. 142; James W., "Pragmatism."

out of the whole number of facts in a situation are rather arbitrarily selected as *the* cause?

The most obvious and nearest incidents impress us as causes, but in reality the situation is not so simple. Especially in the organic and social sciences the number of relevant factors is legion. We may pounce on particulars, but no proof for such cause and effect will be forthcoming. For not only is reproduction of the situation technically impossible, but what is more, we shall not all classify cause and effect in the same way. It is often a case of weighing trained knowledge against amateur views, with the understanding that in the end either may feel right. Where no direct appeal to the senses whose reactions we all share in common is possible, the rule of public opinion or of reputed authority begins.

§ 4. **Causation and Economic History.**— If, now, we apply this analysis of correlation and causation to the Marxian statement of the economic interpretation of history, or to the question of the relation between economic and non-economic facts, we shall see that causal connections such as socialism has commonly asserted do not exist. The economic world embodies stimuli that act upon man, but so do many non-economic facts. And man himself is needed in the situation to give contents to both. The economic facts are part of our thinking and feeling. If any one fact is a cause in such an ensemble it should be man whose mind is a unit, and whose facts of consciousness are all inextricably interwoven.

From the psychological standpoint, that is to say, the Marxian superstructure of law and philosophy is merely a set of interests somewhat farther from the primitive man, from the center of attention and striving, than the acts of production and exchange. Man's needs are graded because of the facts of his evolution and physical constitution. Some of our reactions, correspondingly, will suit the immediate needs of survival or social developments; others may persist even when primary needs catering to survival have changed.

To illustrate. It should not be difficult to trace a connection between prohibition and the value of sobriety in modern production, or between the sanctioning of female modern rights and women's industrial activities, or between our present praise of thrift and the debt of the United States or our fear of propertyless masses. Such "ethical" facts may be thought to rest directly on economic facts, though the causal chain runs both ways. But, on the other hand, the economics of the ancient Hindoos could only faintly be reconstructed from the Vedas. Our idea of Chinese economic environment cannot be properly derived from a study of their voluminous literary works. The art of all ages shows considerable uniformity of ideas and technique, and but little peculiarity indicative of particular modes of living. Similarly with scientific speculation, philosophy, and concepts of government or morality. The principles of sociation which sociology and economics study rest on facts of human nature, and these are so constant that certain rules of conduct are valid for all times, however variable their form and economic expression.

To speak of *interaction* of economic and non-economic facts is chiefly to use a figure of speech, for what is interaction? If I see a cat and dog fighting I can follow the movements of each and see each acting upon the other, with results visible perhaps to the eye. That is interaction in the real sense of the word. But in social affairs the relation is more nearly one of force according to the physicist's use of the term. The physicist can describe force only as a product of two factors; or, to be quite accurate, force to him is simply a ratio, a function of variables. Force refers to couples never reducible to entities. So it is with economic and non-economic aspects. We have never seen them apart. We can only say, as the phychologist sometimes says, that two sets of events move in unison, parallel to each other. Whether interaction in the strict sense of the term takes place he may be loth to decide. He pleads ignorance and goes ahead confident of results from his labors. So with the student of social events. In speaking of their interactions he really has in mind only coexistences which, in any given correlation, appear to him as an organic whole. He cannot reduce it to independent units, though he may picture the parts as functioning like the parts, say, of the human body. The picture helps us to understand, to get meaning out of our words.

But the relation of economic to so-called non-economic events may be still better elucidated by modern psychology, whose conclusions are important for all phases of sociological analysis.

Three fundamental facts need to be remembered in this connection. The first is that *all* objects, not merely the economic, may act as stimuli. The second is the differences in reactions by different men upon like stimuli, or conversely the fact that different men react upon different things.

Our environment may be defined as the things we consciously or unconsciously react upon. It is what we respond to in a physical or mental way that constitutes part of our life, not everything about us in space. Shakespeare, thus, becomes part of my experience, while people still alive, but many miles away and in no wise brought in touch with me personally or indirectly, are strangers that do not figure in my environment. Again, since our life is a cycle of growth and decay, it is natural that at different ages different things should enter into our psychic world. The boy does not see what interests an adult, but he observes much else that grown-ups overlook. Sex and age and profession and congenital proclivities are determinants of environment psychologically viewed.

But from this follows the individuality of thought and feeling, and more especially the independence of both from the external world. Thirdly, then, the *effect of memory and associations stands in no measurable* relation to the objects about us, and furthermore, centrally aroused sensations become more and more important with age and historical development of races, so that correlations between economic data and mentality are altogether indeterminate. One cannot infer from external facts what precise value our thought will take. Inventions, e. g., start commonly with economic facts, but their direction depends on memory associations which in their turn are governed by predisposition, by the laws governing perception, immediate purpose, etc., etc. As the psychologist expresses it: "It is seldom that an act or thought is controlled merely by a single stimulus or even by the stimuli that are being received at the moment of action. The laws of facilitation and inhibition of one set of cortical activities by others that are going on simultaneously in other paths and in other areas are needed if we are to obtain any accurate picture of cortical action,"[15] and that means also of concepts in general. Attitude is a great deal. Whether the picture in the book looks to me like a rabbit or like a duck's bill depends on angle of vision and on subconscious activities within me. The thought of a seismograph on seeing a crisscross of lines may only occur to a person after *other* facts have suggested earth-

15 Pillsbury, W. B., "Fundamentals of Psychology," p. 91.

quakes, as an actual experience has shown. My trend of reasoning and the direction of discovering vary with previous training and general interests. This is the overwhelming evidence of the history of science. *Thoughts have their own history,* and their economic effects are consequents in point of time rather than coexistences, though the historian expands his concept of simultaneity and thus obtains a comparison of economic and non-economic events. "The movement of thought might be regarded as an interaction of purposes and environment, each of which in some measure modifies the other. At least no interpretation and no improvement can be considered as a discrete event. It has its meaning in, and its appearance and development is controlled by, wider mental and physical contexts. These serve to determine the nature of the appreciation and to give the desire that leads to the particular improvements. In this way the progress of thought is one continuous operation. No part can be understood unless it is considered with the whole." [16]

The independence of thought is real. *Economic facts* do not make or mold the non-economic, nor must a history *of religion or of jurisprudence be referred to particular and corresponding economic epochs.* Such a cross reference may form a part of an historical study, but cannot be essential except in a few cases. The study of legislation regulative of economic relations, including property relations, is an economic subject, though legislation is a political function. Politics is the application of the principles of sociology and economics toward social betterment. In this sense jurisprudence and law are best understood in the light of economic data, but this is no instance of the economic man making our non-economic his-

[16] Pillsbury, W. B., "Psychology of Reasoning," p. 286.

tory. It shows the possibility merely of studying economic relations from two view-points, the individual and the collective.

§ 5. **The Law of Maladjustment.**— The Marxian interpretation of history takes due notice of a conflict between individuals and ideas, and makes it the basis for a theory of revolution and progress which is more in accord with scientific thought than his subordination of the intellectual and moral force to the economic. He announced the impending doom of capitalism on two grounds, first because systematic exploitation would ultimately consolidate all property into the hands of a few who, while having no competitors to fear, would be faced by a hungry proletariat that would claim what was rightfully theirs, and secondly because economic and non-economic achievements and norms tend to overlap at certain times, the maladjustment growing until a break was inevitable, which would restore an adjustment between the two fields of thought and action. The exact manner in which this periodic maladjustment is brought about does not appear to have been described anywhere, but one must infer that differences arising between new ideas and old traditions were meant.

In a sociological sense conflicts are ordinarily of two kinds. Men fight each other in the peaceful way that modern economics exemplifies so strikingly, or they are torn by inner conflicts. We either have to contend with others, or with ourselves. The underlying reasons are often the same for both cases, but the feeling created is far from the same. We cannot hate ourselves, though we sometimes think so. On the other hand it is hard to forgive our enemies, though there is much to excuse them. Misery has these aspects. It is objective when disease and poverty stalk among the masses and make their life a burden. It is objective in so far as the economic relations between men have been regulated by laws open to inspection. It becomes subjective when we think of one set of men holding ideas scorned by a second set, the two quarreling about their rights and duties. And it again takes a subjective hue when we look into our own self and find doubt and scruples, ideals falsely focussed, practices incompatible with resolutions made and cherished.

The law of progress enunciated by Marx is a reflex of these several forms of conflict, and it agrees partly with the facts of correlation and causation considered a while ago. Maladjustment does occur pretty regularly. Perhaps it would not be wrong to make it a part of human history as much as reversion is part of evolution. A cutting back is no worse, no more irregular, than a cutting ahead. The recapitulation theory for that reason has been revised by careful biologists.

Conflict always accompanies control, and is a result of two sorts of differences between men, namely those that appear when we compare them at an instant of time, and those due to different *rates* of reaction and growth covering a longer period.

The social process is one of interaction between man and environment. The environment is physical and social, and for reasons already suggested it may at times be advantageous to separate social activities into the economic and non-economic. Physical environments exercise a great influence over men, and they differ from place to place. The environment is chiefly climate, but climate comprises many factors such as temperature, humidity, solar radiation, length of day and season, wind pressure and direction, variability per month and day, extremes of range during the year, the combination of temperature with humidity and wind pressure, and so on. The effect of such variations upon man, and in particular upon labor capacities, has been carefully studied. That climate has much to do with temperament is well known. That literature and art no less than economic achievements or the nature of scientific endeavors bear testimony to the influence of climate has also been admitted for many decades. But it is a more recent opinion that energy and inventiveness are functions of climate, and that the history of civilizations is largely one of climatological changes now hidden from view, but powerful in their day.[17]

Climate is part of latitude and topography, but the latter has direct bearings, too, on the development of transportation and travel. Facilities for communication vary with the lay of the land, with coastal contour and the characteristics of river and lake systems. Mountain ranges and plateaus, drainage basins and passes, the sloping of ranges and their passes, these and other features count in history. They form the outer limits, so to say, beyond which human will dare not move. What the earth provides in minerals and timber, soil fertility and water power, that is a maximum man can seldom ignore. If, therefore, men live in greatly different physical environments their capacities and wants cannot correspond favorably. There will arise opposing viewpoints.

Yet it has been to many thinkers axiomatic that maladjustment is not a product of nature conditions, but instead a social excrescence. Man makes himself miserable; he is not made so by nature. The trouble ordinarily lies then in economic conditions, relative to which differences in physical environs and in human nature may be discounted. Men are congenitally very different and will

[17] See especially Huntington, F., in his "Civilization and Climate," and his more recent: "World Power and Evolution."

never sympathize with each other on all points. They are bound to part company somewhere. So also the differences of climate develop their peculiarities. But we must assume these facts and, making them our constants, attempt to adapt economic facts and personal relations to them. An offsetting policy would be always opportune. If, however, the economic differences in wealth and upbringing, in aptitudes and daily occupation, in modes of living and social control, if these facts, too, separate men, their interests may become irreconcilable.

And to this source of misunderstanding and friction we are bound to add the effect of *different rates of change* in the several factors, physical, personal, and economic.

The physical environment changes but slowly: so slowly that, barring earthquakes and floods or such like, it appears to us stagnant. Only the geologist is interested in the imperceptible movements that are part of our earth's record.

But since men are so differently constituted some will keep abreast of their times, and many will not. The inventive man who helps to reconstruct our economic mechanism is, along some lines, likely to adjust himself to each moment, but to the average man the trend of economic affairs is only a means to greater creature comforts, and beyond that a source of annoyances, his habits being jolted by new demands arising from he wonders where. However, even the innovator, the man chiefly instrumental in translating ideas into a concrete world of goods, will retain many habits as of old, even when they are affected by his own scientific contributions. Man is a unit. Yes. But his mental *associations need not therefore all move on one level.* A master mind in science or merchandising is often a mediocre in his appraisal of non-professional facts. He has for the first score of years been under guidance that impregnated him with ideas not all adaptable to the new conditions which he himself assists in creating. For one thing some memory associations antedate our creative life, and that has profound significance for the facts of maladjustment. And for another thing, even during the creative period of life men remain conservative in many respects. Ideas move in groups. Many groups will not be directly involved in the process of thought filling our professional life. Others will be gradually revised, and some ideals as well as habits will not budge a bit. Thus each man, the most richly gifted not excluded, may be pictured as keeping only here and there pace with his outer world. Ideas radiate changes in many directions, but within us the change moves more nearly in certain specialized fields. The realignment of stimuli from the outside, though forced by our innovations, calls for a wider range of adaptation in response and habits of thinking than we are capable of. The result is a testing within, which may eventually spell skepticism and revolt, misery objective no less than subjective. It is again a matter of difference in degree as between different social groups. None are altogether exempt from the ordeal.

But furthermore, the lines of cleavage socially are accentuated by the power of custom. Custom is habit viewed socially. Habit dies with the individual: custom does not. Custom is opinion preserved and transmitted from generation to generation, the modifications being hardly noticeable, though marked at last. If all men were equally endowed with intelligence and energy custom would be less important and conviction more. But as things are, the norms of a minority are sure to impress the majority, and Personality survives person.

Habits are standardized. Ideals are habits of thought

on certain matters. Ideals are norms governing our conduct, or tending to do so on the average. These norms become frequently traditions handed from father to son, from one age to another. They have been called sanctions because only by popular sanction can these practices in thought and action exercise such control over our lives. Many of these norms are institutionalized in church and school, family and government, or in business etiquette. They envelop us from the very beginning and do not leave us until death. They gather momentum which triumphs over reason. That is to say, just as our strictly personal views and habits are more or less mobile, some making for changes in our environment and some failing to move in unison with them, so social heredity may make a fetich of norms after they have ceased to correspond closely with the world about us. Or, to state the situation differently: Some of our views and habits change more slowly than others, not only by nature, but because of the daily impress of authority from without. The power of parental control should be distinguished from the control of law or government, and the joint effect of all must be compared with the associational process constituting our mental life, which for some is so productive of tangible economic results, while to others it means little — either in creativeness or in feelings of conflict.

If then we speak of being out of harmony with our environment we mean these three things, first that our mental development has progressed unevenly in different directions; secondly that some of us have grown while others have stagnated, content to accept matters as they are, regardless of the demands of the more progressive; and third, that our fellowmen are to us an objective real influence in different degrees.

As to this social environment. In one sense the

phrase "social environment" is inapt, for society is a unit, and from the collectivist standpoint of the sociologist a social environment can only mean society confronted with nature. But that is not the sense in which the phrase is commonly used. So it must express an individual standpoint. The individual calls all his fellowmen his environment. But is this a correct attitude? In so far as all individuals are substantially alike, one cannot make or mar the other. Nature conditions set real limits to human striving, but my average compatriot cannot. Or, at any rate, if he is *my* environment so am I *his*. Hence the term has a dual aspect which may easily be forgotten.

Nevertheless does it refer to something very definite in another sense. For since men are not all equal, since some exercise lasting influence over others it follows that much of the average man's environment is the superior man of talent or genius. To those supermen the social environment is, in its living members, a minor factor, albeit not a negligible one. But to their mediocre contemporaries they themselves are major factors, a social environment in a much more serious sense. The great men originate and propagate ideas. They prescribe rules of conduct, even if the observance thereof rests mainly with the imitators. The supermen alter conditions and often defy the sanctions. They induce the less gifted to question the traditional, perhaps to make sport of long hallowed customs. Thus the course of maladjustment between social groups is hastened, and finally a movement becomes visible whose aim is confessedly the assault upon social heritage. Something like this effect is produced by migrations. If many millions move from one physical and economic environment into a very different, they are likely to receive a shock, because their habits and ideals cannot migrate in the same way. They are firmly lodged and offer a wall of resistance to whatever demands a new outer world makes. The result is disconcerting, and for some individuals may spell disaster. The Scotchman's thrift may look like niggardliness when he migrates from his inhospitable heath to the fertile plains of America. The European who is taught to flatter and fawn if he would succeed, finds his habits unprofitable in a land where mobility of rank and power is no less understood than the mobility of labor and capital.

Maladjustment, however, results from innate predispositions as well as from a conflict of ideas representing different interests acquired during the individual's life. People are congenitally conservative and radical with regard to different norms of living, or some are predominantly conservative while others tend strongly toward radicalism. The conservative clings to existing institutions and customs, and is naturally suspicious of all innovations whose practical value is not immediately apparent. The radical is disposed to doubt the goodness of practices generally approved, but is greatly impressed with the need of reform along intellectual or moral lines. The one type seems to build up only harmonious associations of thought, that lead to further developments of a line of reasoning, but are incapable of reconstruction into new valuations; the other type, on the contrary, means in professional pursuits a novel selection of data and theories, with the result that new vistas of thought are opened up, sometimes perhaps to cause a revolution in science and economic activities.

The radicals are apt to get the worst of it in the early parts of a transition period; the conservatives seem out of place in the latter stages when people have become sufficiently acclimated in a new environment of thought to see the shortcomings of the past. The illadjusted in either case are punished for their minority views when the dominant group of the ruling class objects to them. Imprisonment and fines are ordinary methods of chastisement. Or more frequently still we express our disapproval by dubbing the maladjusted ones iconoclasts and rebels, cranks and fogeys, freaks and maniacs. The innovator in science and art will be put down as a phantast or a charlatan until he has found an audience whose sympathy gives "tone" to his creations. In politics the most defiant of traditions are known as radicals or progressives, or, as nowadays, they become bolshevists whose teachings infuriate the standpatter. But not infrequently such daring spirits have immortalized themselves. They have died on the scaffold only to be praised in song and oratory thereafter. As patriots and fathers of their country some of them have gained undying fame, when during their lifetime they were but an object for derision and slander. In all fields of achievement this turn-about in valuations has repeatedly come, and it will come again. The daring business man who at the outset seemed a crackbrained plunger makes good eventually as pioneer and founder of a firm. The visionaries and the heretics who become respectively prophets and saints, the rebel whose treason inspires later generations, — they are all examples of maladjustment brought about by large social movements.

§ 6. **The Theory of Prosperity.**— However, though overlappings of ideals new and old occur continually, this does not do away in the slightest degree with the reality of an objective standard for measuring welfare. The economic interpretation, on the contrary, includes such a test, and the Marxian view implies it even though the idea was not anywhere elaborated. Human history, from this standpoint, has meant for the most part progress and social betterment. In spite of recurring periods of maladjustment the trend has been steadily toward the attainment of a higher plane of prosperity. The world is truly becoming better, and social science, having established its norm, may consciously promote the wellbeing of men. It would be fatal for us to assent to John Stuart Mill's dictum that "questions of ultimate ends are not amenable to direct proof. Whatever can be proved to be good must be so by being shown to be a means to something admitted to be good without proof."[18] If he were correct in believing that "the sole evidence it is possible to produce that anything is desirable is that people do actually desire it"[19]— if this were so, then social science in a very serious sense had lost its mission.

The failure of utilitarianism as once understood is clearly presaged in this essay of a mighty thinker. However, on the one hand, we are convinced these days that Mill himself need not have rejected the economic tests because he started with pleasure and pain, and on the other hand it is not necessary to abjure all personal tests because of a social approach to the problem.

The objective tests of prosperity may be given first consideration even if we feel bound to believe in an Absolute such as happiness, pleasure, salvation of the soul, godliness, etc. It is essentially a question of coupling a measurable sort of welfare with the immeasurable. The concepts of a supreme good which the Asiatics and Greeks first formulated, and whose history is virtually the history of all speculative thought, do not lend themselves to measurement. We cannot tell when a man is happy; we cannot measure different amounts of pleasure and pain,

[18] Mill, J. S., "Utilitarianism," Chapter 1.
[19] *Ibidem,* Chapter 4.

though the hedonists once hoped to find principles for measurements. It is impossible to gauge the goodness of a man if his innermost creed as to world and infinity is to serve as a criterion. The salvation of the soul may be the greatest of human achievements and the sine qua non of peace here on earth, but its roots and course of development escapes our vigilance, no matter how we watch it. Old norms then have failed in the sense that we have not been able to prove their existence in individual cases, nor found any means of measuring them and comparing them. It is not an unreasonable conjecture to make, seeing what we know of the evolution of men, that the cavedweller was as happy or as good, in the conventional ethical sense, as the modern man. But if we compare their respective achievements and social organization, or if we should be able to test their respective efficiency and modes of living, the gains of civilization would stand out boldly enough. The poorest may be happy and virtuous, if the two words are defined suitably, but so may the wealthy and proficient, the healthy and intelligent.

An idiot is guiltless? Probably. But we do not therefore put him on a par with the gifted. The sick are good and willing? No doubt, but their pains and foibles embarrass them nonetheless. The paupers have merry moments and cultivate their soul? Certainly, but their distress is real for all that, calling for redress on the part of a legislator or friend who would add health, wealth, and efficiency to all the possible kinds of goodness the human mind has dreamed of. The need of an empirical and economic standard of prosperity is therefore our need for a goal, in the attainment of which society at large shall rest satisfied and strong. The need is for the possession of goods that make possible learning and leisure, variety of experience and a full mete of self-realization.

The functions of an economic concept of prosperity may be illustrated from the relation of art to life. Art is an ideal as well as a fact taking sens-ible forms. Art has always been lauded as one of the highest manifestations of reason and genius. The world has produced much art, and certain nations have excelled in wonderful creations of music or painting, architecture, literature, and sculpture. But the criteria of art are elusive. What is real art and what is banality or shallow imitation few will decide. Opinions are nowhere more subjective than in the realm of art where canons change continually.

Art also has no value at a supreme moment, in a struggle of nations, in the contest between social groups fighting for power and happiness as they understand them. The nations most productive of art have had their ascendancy and their decline. A people totally devoid of art may easily score a victory over a foe than whom none has achieved finer things judged æsthetically. The vulgar view of art, then, is at odds with man's intense desire for life and supremacy. Art goes for nought when a battle opens.

The ethical norms, too, may appear inferior to none, but if they do not issue in appropriate social expression they leave no impress. Whether a group or a nation shall live depends on its equipment in peace and war, on its treasure of goods, their volume and nature, their distribution and use. He who is healthy has an advantage over the ailing. He who has wealth is better off than the poor, if otherwise their lots are equal. He who can do things is superior to the helpless and ignorant.

But the economic norm of prosperity is social. Only for *large groups of people* living together can efficiency, health, and wealth be tested. Individual training is not the only factor of importance in the productiveness of a nation, as history has shown from earliest days on. As soon as individual self-sufficiency came to an end, as a result of the economies of division of labor, proficiency took on a social meaning. Thereafter the usefulness of a man was shown best when he produced jointly with others.

And so with health and wealth. They count most when related to communities as a whole, to nations and races. Wars are won by nations whose social organization permits them, in various ways, to promote the norms of prosperity more generally than their opponents are capable of.

Virtue is, at a crucial moment, good citizenship. It points to the right place for the individual among his fellowmen whose wellbeing is ordinarily his own. Such virtues are consequently measurable by particular forms of conduct. We can tell whether a man has sinned against the rules of health and efficiency when we have no means of finding out whether he believes all that's in a catechism.

Wealth in tangible goods is as essential to progress as it is fit for measurement and comparison. The inherent ingenuity of man accounts for the first steps toward civilization, but once wealth was acquired it became a further guarantee of progress. For surplus means leisure and increasing specialization of workers, and this in turn enhances social productiveness. Education is impossible without leisure. The modern forms of research could not continue if our regular surplus of goods were suddenly to disappear. Much work would then stop. Production itself, however, necessitates also technical coöperation, a corollary of which is a sense of interdependence and a social conscience, that is a feeling of worth in our fellowmen, our rivals or friends. Wealth brings cumulatively the means of communication which perpetuate knowledge and help disseminate it among the masses. And since the power of our association of ideas varies largely with their range and character, early training and selection become important. Thus methods of production stand in some ratio to existing wealth. We learn to "find" ourselves, to trace correlation expressive of health and illness. Our hygienic and sanitary measures are prophylactic as well as corrective. The general round of wealth, leisure, knowledge, proficiency, health, vigor, and production repeats itself endlessly. There is no other way of attaining prosperity than the economic, though we may translate this into visions of personal value, into precepts of conduct sanctioning what the biological and psychological facts have already urged. The sociologist, thus, will utilize their data for purposes of understanding social intercourse in general, but the economist has to *add the rules* of production and exchange by which wealth, health, and efficiency are procured most abundantly.

§ 7. Summary on the Economic Interpretation of History.— To conclude. The economic interpretation of history comprises several noteworthy points. First, the tracing of a causal relation between economic and non-economic events is an idle undertaking because all life is a unit and all economics the product of a mental unit: man himself. The concept of causation is evidence merely of our penchant for selection and concentration. All events are interrelated, but it is as correct to write a history of religion without resort to economics as to record economic developments without injecting a dissertation on religion. The precise bearing of one on the other is a rather personal matter.

In the second place, the sufficiency of a purely empirical viewpoint cannot be doubted. We can never do without premises in one respect, but all the attempts of the metaphysician have presumed upon our credulity by taking for granted much of what was to be explained and proven. Socialism has done better, therefore, by confining its investigations to a world realistically conceived and familiar to all. The materialistic viewpoint has proven useful, for it has helped us to think of society as governed by fundamental instincts instead of its being the pet of Providence.

In the third place, maladjustment is a regular part of life springing from the very foundations of human nature and its relation to a changeable environment. We shall perhaps never eliminate it completely. For this reason alone, if for no other, the Marxian aim at a millennium must lead to disillusionment. Misery, tho best understood as a social excrescence, is yet something for which science has so far found no single antidote. We cannot expect a cure by one step, nor a curing of evils by one means applied to all times.

In the fourth place, the facts of biological and social sciences lead us to the adoption of a utilitarian standpoint, but utility is then not defined as pleasure or absence of pain. The norms of welfare are not individual whose aggregate sums make prosperity for the nation at large. Our norms, rather, must be objective even for the individual. Not his feelings, but facts of health, wealth, and efficiency decide the question. In part individually, in part socially measurable, they tell us what degree of wellbeing a people has reached, and how it compares with other social units. Correspondingly virtue is not creed, but conduct. The test of virtue is not suffering, as the Flagellants and like-minded folk preached, but service, as taught by the Christ.

The economic interpretation of history comprises this

view of goodness and righteousness. It embraces the whole field of conduct associated formally with ethics, and logically compels socialism to redefine justice. Prosperity is the result of just relations between men, but that they are just is shown by the objective realities studied chiefly by economists.

CHAPTER V

JUSTICE

§ 1. **The Principle of Differentiation.**— The founders of socialism said little about justice, but a great deal about the evils of an unequal distribution of wealth. They were interested in the principles of sociation and of economics, not in abstract questions of right and wrong. Their works abound in passages criticizing theoretical positions of an opponent, while to the sentimental pleadings of the utopians they turned a deaf ear. Since then the attitude of socialists has remained about the same. They have insisted on an objective treatment of sociological subjects. They have sought to lay bare the foundations of the social structure rather than launch reforms from a sense of morality or fair dealing. Scientific socialism has endeavored to understand the laws of nature rather than individualistic concepts of justice and goodness.

Yet the definition of justice is a corollary to the economic interpretation of history proclaimed by Marx and Engels, and the idea of a better world in which equity should rule for the protection of all is really prominent in the teachings of socialism. What is popularly separated from matters of fact as a distinct question of ethics has been by socialists incorporated with social science. Ethics and economics have been fused into one single topic. There is no way of answering the questions first put by Marx without reaching also some definite conclusions on the ends of government and the nature of justice.

But the definition is implied rather than stated in so many words. And again, the modern view of history or of social processes and of prosperity does away with the old-time notion of a distinct science of ethics detachable from social sciences, such as sociology and economics are. Justice cannot be defined in general terms. To try it is even less profitable than defining fundamentals in other sciences. As soon as we seek to embrace all in a single sentence we lose the meaningfulness of words. They become nondescript and unsatisfactory to all but a few of the initiated. And to them the broadest definitions are useful only because supported by a wealth of particulars held in the background of consciousness.

What is justice? The definition would resemble the vagueness of definitions on matter and force, life and space, electricity and motion, mind and value and time. We define such words, but make mental reservations. Our ideas change, and we have to redefine. Science changes its point of view and stresses new facts. The life of a thinker is a quest for definitions. He would give contents to the vehicles of expression that the man on the street uses so lightly. It is the mark of a thinking man that he knows what his words mean, and differentiates nicely between their exact meanings. But the largest concepts cannot be defined so as to have lasting value for science. Justice may be defined a half a dozen ways without giving us an idea of its relation to everyday experience. Justice should be referred to particulars.

There is another approach to the problem of justice which agrees well with the scientific viewpoint of socialism. We may go over all the cases of justice or injustice that we can remember, and we shall then notice that the question always turns on a comparison of inequalities.

Life is nothing if not inequalities as to things, and between men. No two things are exactly alike. This is a trite saying. Differences are the rule, and resemblances are only of a degree. In physical environment, in the characters of men, and in the institutions of society the fact of inequality attracts our attention.

The world's resources for instance are very unequally divided between nations, some having an abundance of mineral and good soil, and others practically nothing of either. The Eskimo might compare his fate with the Frenchman's or American's, and bewail his fate. Or the Patagonian might gaze with envy upon the riches bestowed by nature upon his northern neighbors in the Argentine. Races in prehistoric times settled in different parts of the globe, or migrated several times since then. They cannot be said to have chosen their abode with an eye to resources excepting fertility of soil, for the kinds of wealth which are now prized most highly were then unknown as an instrument for progress. It is chance that gave to some great resources, while others were allotted a meager store of bare necessities.

So with the differences among humans. Sex itself is a differentiation of far reaching import. We might compare the characteristic activities, the burdens and privileges, of male and female and find much that seems unjust in a sense. At times we have been so told. Or there are race traits to compare; the superiorities of a white man over the Hottentot and the mode of living which, in part resulting from these differences, drives the two groups far apart. History is colored deeply by racial characteristics. It is folly to overlook them in a larger survey.

And what of the inborn differences traced to heredity or to variation? What of the strong in body and mind, and the frail? What of the subnormal and the super-normal, the types of personality that are to be met everywhere in life? The variety is bewildering and is said to lend charm to life. Probably so. But the fact of such differences remains and cannot be attributed to any particular, measurable action of those possessing the advantages or the handicaps. We simply accept the differences. We know that some are born lucky and others unlucky. We know that some will struggle throughout life without achieving anything unusual, while others will succeed virtually without effort. We know that the pretty girl is surrounded by admirers and looks forward to all sorts of blessings, when her less comely sister is left to walk alone. We know that some will work creatively and reap rewards, while the less gifted but perhaps more industrious will live in penury, forgotten and cheerless.

History is itself a record of differences sometimes appalling to behold. What cruelties and hardships have befallen millions of innocent people! We read of catastrophes wiping out the lives of thousands. We hear of cripples and the demented, or of miserable wretches stricken with loathsome diseases. We read that an explosion has killed so many miners in a second. We think of the wars that have killed and maimed hundreds of millions for no reason except that life seems to be a battle in which some fight and suffer more than others. We turn the pages of a History of the World and are impressed with nothing so much as with the inequalities of men and their fates. And many have endured horrible pains. Indeed, one might add that the path of human progress is strewn with the wrecks of men and women who suffered without guilt. Some were put to horrible tortures or consigned to the flames. Some were immured alive or flayed to death. Some died on the rack, and others were butchered as a sacrifice to false gods. Many perished from famine, and others again fell a prey to wild beasts. If differences as such are to count in the problem of justice, why should we not muse over the mysteries of Fate that let some live amidst the comforts of the twentieth century while the great majority lived a coarse struggling life in the earlier stages of human development? As the believer in justice sees it, these differences form a disenchanting chapter in the history of the world.

And yet this is not all. For we have still two other types of disparity to remember, to wit, the socio-economic stratification, and the suffering of the innocent for the guilty.

As to the former, the evidence is about us abundantly. It forms the chief theme of reformers, and is a cardinal point in the program of socialism. The world's goods, they say, are too unevenly divided. Some are born rich and others never save a penny. Some toil but remain poor, while others bask in affluence without turning a finger. As goods are distributed, so are the pleasures and privileges that money can buy or that it procures indirectly. It is for some to walk in the best of society — however understood — and to shape the destiny of millions, while the multitude follows and sees little of what their age represents. Some will shoulder burdens to relieve others who tread lightly and carefree. In a war, for instance, one group goes to the front, perhaps never to return, or worse yet, to return crippled and helpless. But another group stays at home because its services are needed there, or for some less pressing reason. The stay-at-homes may be getting their deserts, but note that they live in comforts and grow rich while their compatriots go into a living death. And often the brave are slain, and the pretenders thrive. How common indeed that heroes are buried by hypocrites!

The innocent also get the worst of it when the offender goes scot free. We see defenseless nations insulted and abused by unscrupulous neighbors, by the Goliaths who are itching for a fight. We see a neutral nation pay for the follies of the combatants. We see a whole nation suffer for the wrongs of its government which after all is not truly representative. Or perhaps the children pay for the sins of their fathers, or we must make good the losses incurred by careless friends.

All this and more is common knowledge. The inequalities have always existed and must be expected to recur on general principles of induction. We cannot eradicate all of them. There are some beyond our control, as well as others that we may consider the expressions of will on the part of men.

We shall have to discriminate but we shall also feel compelled to admit that life without inequalities is unthinkable. The task of the reformer is not the uniformization, but the *coördination of specialized forms of living* so that the largest number of people may live in relative peace and contentment. Not a leveling for its own sake, but leveling with a view to progress, this is the task before us. To level rights and duties for classes of people rather than for all people, this must be our aim. Differentiations are the prime characteristic of life, and the price of evolution. We cannot abolish them. But we can divide society into groups with specialized functions, and then assign to each its burdens and privileges. Equality for all *in a given class*, such leveling is feasible. Equal rights for all members in a certain occupational class, or of an age group, or per sex, or relative to civic status, and so on. This is the sort of uniformity compatible with economic advancement and urged by our objective norms of prosperity. All self-imposed or socially induced forms of pain should be eliminated.

§ 2. **The Nature of Justice.**— Such a view of equalization suggests also several negative answers to the problems of justice. It is clear, for instance, that the promise of heavenly rewards cannot hush the protests of the unlucky, for according to this promise the fortunate here on earth will fare equally well in the hereafter. Where, then, is the logic of inequality during this life?

Again, justice cannot be called rightly an institution of nature, as was held by the ancients and by philosophers since. This idea that nature is peace and happiness, and society a decline and fall from virtue, is pure superstition, however revered it may be by some who are more influenced by religious promptings than by facts. There is nothing to show that the jungle life is more pleasant than ours. On the contrary, we have proof of its being everywhere a harsh struggle, and most so among the brutes. Nature has not set the table for men. What they want they must for the most part earn. Life is a battle, not a frolic and minstrel show. The naturalistic view of origins of injustice is as fanciful as its conclusions on the founts of constitutional government.

In the third place, we may also be sure that norms of equity cannot be based on mere intuitions. No more than men by nature are altruistic are they capable of distinguishing between right and wrong. The history of morals, which has been studied by many men with great diligence, shows the relativity of ethical norms and the immense variety of conceptions on right and wrong. At different times different codes of conduct have arisen. Any one who observes has profited in this respect from his travels. We see much dissension among people on identical points. Customs vary, and laws reflect the economic setting of officially sanctioned demands for justice. Laws cannot be understood to make justice, for what is held just at one time may become unsatisfactory long before the lawmaker adapts himself to the change. This phase of maladjustment has been discussed in an earlier chapter. Laws do not create justice, but they give evidence of norms accepted by people as right or fair. Law is a derivative whose original is science or the *mores* or the standard set by exceptional men.

Justice, then, is this one positive thing, whatever else may be said about it: Justice refers to human institutions and to facts of life unknown to barbarism. Justice is an ideal presupposing a reasoning man, a willing being, a responsible being. Justice is for thinking men on an advanced level of living. Only when somehow we believe ourselves as individuals capable of willed action, only when we possess the ability to foresee certain events or to master a set of relations, only then are we fit to develop a notion of justice and to govern ourselves accordingly. Justice is a general policy comprising actions suited to reason and responsibility. The things we can control become subjects for reform. The facts utterly beyond our guidance we leave out of the equation. Justice always is a social norm that deals with the relations between thinking and striving members of a large whole. That is just which subserves the end of the largest possible number, after the end has been defined according to the dictates of social science. Justice is an ideal of social relations and of aims *varying with times.*

"Right," the author of "Folkways" informs us, "can never be natural, or God-given, or absolute in any sense. The morality of a group at a time is the sum of the —

folkways by which right conduct is defined. Therefore morals can never be intuitive. They are historical, institutional, and empirical."[1] The just act is one which is conducive to the welfare of the largest possible number, welfare having previously been rated by the economic tests compared to which all other norms are subjective and incapable of measurement. "The problem of morality is the formation, out of the body of original instinctive impulses which compose the natural self, of a voluntary self in which *socialized* desires and affections are dominant, and in which the last and controlling principle of deliberation is the love of the objects which will make this transformation possible."

We repeat, justice has connotations of reason and responsibility socially utilized. Irrational people cannot be expected to deal squarely with their fellowmen. Or, since this test of reason itself is the power of coördinating efforts, we had better admit that justice *is* reason, and that the objective tests of social welfare furnish the best proof for the existence of either. When society progresses and the need of the average man is reflected in the strength of the larger unit, then justice prevails. It is justice in the long run, in large categories, in vital affairs that matters. Sacrifices of self and of detail is inseparable from justice properly conceived. "Justice may be defined as such an adjustment of the conflicting interests of the citizens as will interfere least with, and contribute most to, the strength of the nation."[2] The *might of the many, measured in terms of health, wealth and efficiency, is the sole available proof of the general prevalence of justice.* And in a struggle between different social groups or between nations it will appear soon enough as to where

[1] Sumner, W. G., "Folkways," p. 29.
[2] Carver, Th. N., "Essays in Social Justice," p. 9.

justice has asserted itself most completely. There are degrees of justice from the social standpoint, whatever our opinion about justice in a particular. We may consider a man either right or wrong, a verdict either just or unjust, disdaining to bicker about shades and shares. But since justice is for individual cases and since life comprises so many duties and rights it is inevitable that, while in some respects we are just to each other, in others we are not. The ideals of politics and economics center about such weighing of pros and cons, our choice finding expression in social structure and economic or military power.

Grant the will-to-live, and you must grant the worth of social strength. Grant reason in man and you will want to hold him responsible for his action. Grant norms of conduct however evolved or formulated, and you will consult them before long when passing judgment on particulars. Will is assumed as a means of eliminating the unfit. The freedom of the will is a tactical device by which we can compare the good with the bad and endeavor an adjustment of conflicting wishes.[3] Will is basic to justice, just as the law of averages is back of our notion of the ought. But will, the psychologist knows, is the subjective aspect of a condition as suitable for examination as the facts of motion. To say that one ought to do a certain thing merely means that *as a rule* such acts will prove beneficial according to definition, or that out of a hundred men, put in a given situation, a certain percentage would act as the particular one "ought to." What the majority does conformable to the needs of society, to needs that sometimes are objectively verifiable

3 Mill, J. S., in his "Logic" (Book Six, Chapter 2, No. 2) gives a definition of determinism which seems still the most lucid and comprehensive of many offered by logicians.

and measurable but at other times are accepted by reasoning from analogy without careful testing, that becomes moral. The injunction to act, the assertion that a certain thing ought to *be* or ought to be *done*, rests on a belief that in most cases justice will thereby triumph.

The much mooted topic of motives versus results loses its vexatious character when treated as a matter of averages. If, e. g., I am instrumental in a child being run over through my attempting to save it from that very fate, the result is taken to be an exception to the rule. Extenuating circumstances will be pleaded because I acted in good faith, i. e., with the intention of saving the child from impending danger. It will be argued that in most cases such a policy on my part brings good results, and that consequently my failure in a particular instance is a contingency to be reckoned with. The principle is deemed more vital than any one application of it, be it successful or not. Thus the law may condemn me, but my sin is pardonable in the eyes of most witnesses. Lenient treatment will be urged.

Motives, therefore, assume a moral aspect only in the sense that they are forecasts of events which in themselves are either social or anti-social. If the former, motives are excusable though leading to undesirable results in one instance; if the latter, motives are reprehensible though leading accidentally to good results. Motives in this respect are like efforts spent in doing a piece of work. I may work hard and get results not commensurate with my efforts and unsatisfactory by objective tests. My reward will agree with the net result, not with the labor expended. But in the long run, it is true, a man is the more likely to accomplish great things, the harder he tries, the more tireless his striving. Hence it is not unfair or illogical to rate men somewhat by their tenacity and diligence.

§ 3. **Justice and Competition.**— If we apply this maxim of average results and of reasoning by analogy, for an individual act, to the relation between religion and economics, or of might to right, we shall be able to solve what otherwise may appear an unsolvable proposition.

It has often been argued that Christianity, for instance, is irreconcilable with economics or with common practice, and similarly that socialism is incompatible with religion. However, the antinomy is not one given by two contrasting viewpoints, but rather it results from one-sided interpretations and abstractions.

The Christian creed is of course a mixture of many tenets not all of which belong to the Gospel as originally preached so far as historical investigation has been able to ascertain. We have the eschatology and the golden rule, the one chiefly, though not entirely, developed after the death of the founder of Christianity, and the other antedating even the advent of the Christ.

The preachings on a monotheistic world order, on an absolute God, his fatherhood, and the endowment of man by God with faculties of reason and with infallible intuitions of right and wrong, these teachings which are grouped about the doctrine of an immortal soul and redemption by proxy may be conveniently detached from the moral code. The Sermon on the Mount has a value independent of the theological superstructure. The idea of a forgiving father and of a final court of appeal above human jurisdiction anchors deep in the human breast. It will be true in all ages that the leveling of rights as preached in the brotherhood of men has salutary social effects. It is an axiom, also, among scientists that their own conclusions are subject to error and to occasional correction, and that all inquiries of the mind have limits beyond which men may still hope and aspire to unknown things.

But on the other hand, the moral precepts of all great religious teachers have been one-sided. They have looked to only one out of several relations existing with regard to any problem. Thus the precepts of Christianity are bold abstractions from concrete instances. They are the fruit of reasoning by analogy. For instance, it is good to treat others as we would treat our own self, but, to begin with, human nature is not altogether of that inclination, and in the second place a rigid regard for this ruling would lead not infrequently to self-effacement. Biologists are not sure that evolution could have operated exclusively on that principle.

The way out of the apparent conflict between religion and reality is not a campaign for changing human nature, but a return to other facts in the situation, and to a reconstruction of our religious beliefs. There is a social basis for religion. In the measure that our abstractions are reconverted to the concrete conditions whence they sprang shall we succeed in uniting theory and practice without destroying the social fabric. Economics, for instance, will be able to adopt a collectivistic viewpoint without ceasing to be scientific if it abandons some of its problems which an earlier age, before natural and social sciences had far progressed, had set, and if it subordinates ethics to social science instead of borrowing from metaphysicians. The stand taken by classic economics toward questions of morality, which once were associated with metaphysics, is responsible for the seeming heartlessness which some critics detected in professional economists. It made John Ruskin say: "I neither impugn nor doubt the conclusion of the science [he refers to economics], if its terms are accepted. I am simply uninterested in them, as I should be in those of a science of gymnastics which assumed that men had no skeletons."[4] It elicited from Carlyle the characteristic exclamation: "All this Mammon Gospel of Supply and Demand, Competition, Laissez Faire, and the Devil take the hindmost, begins to be one of the shabbiest Gospels ever preached, or altogether the shabbiest."[5]

The "economic man" was somewhat of an abstraction, but even more so is the definition of justice and of the ultimate good whose study the economists wished to leave to another line of thinking.

Competition need not be what the "dismal science" made it. It need not incite the admirer of the Christian creed to the thought that "competitive industry and commerce are based on selfishness as the dominant instinct and duty, just as Christianity is based on love."[6] If the fault were as grave as pictured, if "our whole socio-economic structure rests theoretically upon the appeal to the selfish —,"[7] then socialism would logically be the only alternative to individualism.

It may be so anyhow, though for different reasons. But recent interpretations of fair competition have suggested a way out, and the conception of the Ought as an estimate of average results desirable to society as a whole, does a similar service.

Competition has by the courts been considered fair when, first, the inequalities between competing parties are

[4] Ruskin, J., in his "Unto This Last."

[5] Carlyle, Th., "Essays, Past and Present: The Working Aristocracy."

[6] Rauschenbusch, W., "Christianity and the Social Crisis," p. 310. See also the same author's "Christianizing the Social Order."

[7] Murdoch, J. G., "Economics as a Basis of Living Ethics," p. 47.

natural, as for instance the innate differences of ability and temperament, or when secondly, the differences arise accidentally, as at the outbreak of the war, which gave some dealers a great advantage over those not stocked up with European products; or in the third place, when the differences are not sufficiently great to make the result of the struggle between rivals a foregone conclusion, or when, in the fourth place, the price and quality alone decide in the sale of goods; or when, finally, goods are marketed by rivals at a price which generally speaking yields a profit permitting of a continuance of business.

To define competition as "fair" under such circumstances is to admit the impossibility of equalizing all facts. It does not dictate an abandonment of the principle of striving among producers and consumers, but it hints at limitations that in the long run safeguard both competitor and the public.

Some sort of inequality and hence of injustice, as popularly understood, is bound to linger among us. Right cannot be right to all contending parties. Might always exists, if by that term we mean the superiority in some respects of force over mere good will, or of law over common sense.

§ 4. **Might versus Right.**— But if we inspect the matter of might versus right more closely we shall find that might means nothing except by reference to something else. Might may mean either muscular strength or mechanical power, or such brain powers as are exercised individually or by dint of social organization. If the force is physical the individual ordinarily is the active agent, as when pugilists settle a question of superiority. Nations also fight, though armies nowadays represent much more than skill or muscle strength. In all such cases might may consist of physical force only, and it deserves mention that ultimately all other values will stand or fall according to the issue of a physical combat.

But manifestly such struggles have nothing to do with social values unless we first posit the latter as occasion for the former. Might strictly speaking is right only when a predominating opinion cannot be upheld by physical force. In that case our disappointment is voiced in the remark that might has triumphed over right. When expert opinion is defied, or the will of the majority is disobeyed (particularly on the confession of the offender himself) then his exercise of physical power is reproved.

Might is right, therefore, when the majority sanctions the force used to uphold its views, whether science supports public opinion or not; or when in the absence of any social values physical force alone governs; or when, in the third place, approved norms of conduct prevail independent of physical coercion. In the long run the will of the majority, however inspired, carries the day. Right, consequently, must triumph as a general rule even though for groups of people and for limited periods of time conditions may be at variance with public opinion.

The law of approximations and of averages thus equates the two sides of right and might for the same reason that it brings into logical relation the fields of religion and of social science, or of economics and of ethics. There is no impassable gulf between socialism — even as taught by Marx — and the religious beliefs. It is not necessary to oust competition from the field of economic endeavor. But on the other hand it is doubtful whether a categorical exclusion of the collectivistic standpoint from economic science will further the interests of economics itself. Justice must be socially conceived and measured. Socialism has first called attention to the need of such a gauging of right and wrong. The future development of social science seems bound to fuse ethics and economics into one single problem, so that people will more nearly than at the present be in accord with scientific conclusions.

CHAPTER VI

THE LIMITS IN PRODUCTION

§ 1. **National Income and Consumption of Goods.**—The path to progress is through plenty. There is no way in which the condition of the average man can be bettered except we raise his income first. Whatever the limitations of mere wealth may be, if we have no wealth, if mankind lives uncertainly from hand to mouth, everything else will also be lacking that is typical of a civilized state. All history so far has forced us to take this attitude. Human development from beginning to end has been a piling up of economic goods the consumption of which has been accompanied regularly by advances in art and science, in speculation and moral judgments.

It is then no trifle if socialism declares to have found a short cut to wealth. If it is true that national income may be greatly increased by abolishing private property we should favor the revolution even though it entail much personal effort and sacrifice. If, as an eminent socialist leader avers, "the transformation of the capitalist system of production into the socialist system must inevitably result in a rapid increase of the quantity of wealth produced"[1] an important question is happily settled. The raising of the general level of living is the concern of all statesmen and reformers. Nothing is so palpably desirable as a doubling of wages, if by it we mean a doubling of the average person's purchasing power.

[1] Kautsky, K., "Class Struggle," a running commentary on the Erfurt Program of the German Sozial-demokratische Partei, translated by Bohn, W. E., p. 145.

Socialism hopes to accomplish this miracle in two ways, namely first by augmenting the national aggregate of goods, and secondly by changing the *ratio* in which necessities and luxuries are now commonly turned out. The first is no doubt the more important step in the long run, but the second could be attempted at shorter notice. And it deserves mention again that this change is to concern, not the monetary values in which we now measure wealth, but the latter itself, that is the amount by weight or volume of the goods that enter into the market. Let the tons or quarts or cubic feet of consumables be doubled or tripled, that is the proposition before us.

We may introduce the nature of this problem by making a distinction between consumables and non-consumables which also figure in the national dividend.

People have often referred to the income, in dollars and cents, of the American nation, with the idea of showing how the average man would fare if the principle of equality were applied. It has been pointed out that, on such a basis, the laborer would have perhaps twice as much as he enjoys to-day. If the total national income in 1918, for instance, amounted to $75,000,000,000 and we assume a population of one hundred million, then the per capita income averaged $750. For a family of five that would mean $3,750, a sum certainly not earned by most families, though enormously below what the richest can boast of.

Such a view, however, is from the very outset misleading because a nation's total annual output of goods is not so to be divided. There are three kinds of funds to be taken into consideration, only one of which becomes available for personal use. The first is the fund needed to replace capital goods worn out in the process of production, or otherwise subject to deterioration. The second is our savings fund which normally swells our national wealth and makes industrial growth as well as a rising level of living, that is a rising fund of consumables, possible. And the third only, namely the consumables just alluded to, constitute the real income which people have in mind when wishing for greater riches. A loaf of bread is part of my consumables. The service rendered by actors whose art I see displayed on the moving picture screen is another such item of income for personal use. Many properties held by governments, though used collectively, serve the same purpose.

But the replacing of capital used in the production of consumables does not gratify me in the same sense, nor is the surplus devoted to the enlargement of capital a genuine part of my income. They are merely means to an end which, at last analysis, is national development. The relative size of the shares varies with the economic resources of the country, with its stage of economic development, growth of population, habits of living, etc. A land richly endowed with resources can evidently maintain a high level of living and yet set aside a large surplus. A country poor in resources may save a relatively large portion of the total income by consuming little. Frugal habits may lead either to a rapidly growing population, or to the accumulation of an investment fund which may be placed either abroad or at home. If resources are lacking it is not likely that the surplus will be large, nor that it finds employment at home. In general the surplus is the larger the greater the total national income, and the replacement fund will grow of course more or less proportionate to the growth of investments. In "young" countries where resources are plentiful and labor scarce the level of living will be high if reckoned by foodstuffs, but low by other standards.

Capital will be imported, that is machinery and ideas will be bought at a high interest rate. The interest will be paid in rawstuffs and rights to natural resources, or the payment will be postponed until suitable consumption goods can be added to the export of raw materials. In such countries the investment fund will grow more rapidly than the flow of consumers' goods, while advanced stages of economic development usually mean a relatively large fund of consumption goods. Legislation, however, may regulate the ratios somewhat so as to promote the interests of the largest number. It is possible to neglect the cultivation of the soil in an endeavor to multiply industrial goods or personal services. In the United States the recent trend has been toward a rapid industrialization of capital. The farmer received probably less than his share. The consumer consequently could not keep as good a table as formerly, though he gained in other directions. It is for the government or the individual to decide which is the more preferable, cheap food or a variety of industrial goods and of services.

Socialism will no doubt decide in favor of foods before investing heavily in the industries. The aim of socialists is to raise the income of the poor. If then — to return to our little problem — we must deduct some fifteen billion dollars a year for replacing worn out capital and expanding business we get instead of $750 per capita only $600 annually in consumables. To raise this, so that the masses will have what ten per cent. now get, means not only to increase the national aggregate, but also to change the ratios of investment, replacements, and consumption funds in some measure. This socialism hopes to do. It will try to better conditions by substituting necessities for luxuries as well as by adding to the total.

§ 2. **What Determines National Income.**— Now production depends on three factors, namely, on natural resources, labor-supply, and efficiency. It is by whatever changes will occur in these factors that socialism will bring about the betterment of income. If it can add to our resources, if it can increase the stock of labor-power either by adding to the number of workers or by lengthening the work-day, and if in the third place it can make men more proficient, whether as individuals or as cogs in a great industrial machine, then its promises of a higher level of living may be fulfilled. If not, the promises can mean nothing.

The answer to our question is not, however, easily given, for the data at hand are extremely limited and not always reliable. It is only with reference to the labor supply that our information is approximately correct. Possible gains or losses in social efficiency cannot be deduced directly from statistics on education or health or socialistic programs, and the effect of socialism on natural resources can be stated only negatively.

It is certain that socialism cannot *produce* natural resources. It can only look for them and then use them. But since socialists have not claimed a greater ability in locating resources than our experts possess now the chief question is that of using them.

The producer distinguishes between physically existent resources and those he can exploit at prevailing prices. He will not work a mine if the vein is too thin or the ore of low yield. He will keep his property but wait for rising prices. When demand has increased and prices rise faster than expenses he is likely to reach for his reserve stocks. He will work less rich tracts of land or deposits of coal and ore if he has to, provided his own profits are not diminished materially. This principle of diminishing returns governs all production and is respected by socialists.

On the other hand they urge that much land and other riches are withheld that should be used now. They argue that to increase these stores is part of their program, and that they will enlarge our resources in the sense that they will not wait for profits as the capitalist undoubtedly does. Let us grant the proposition and add temporarily ten per cent. to our productive power by this route. Yet it deserves noting that the gain will be only temporary. For competitive principles will make an end of speculative reservations sooner or later. In Europe the idea of waste through disuse could hardly come in question. In the United States, indeed throughout the world, the tendency is steadily toward exploitation of what is in sight. Either, therefore, the gain has been of brief duration or we face the still less pleasant fact that we may hasten development unnecessarily.

Socialism deals with long stretches of time. It is not interested merely in the immediate future. It will not care, therefore, to raise our level of living by working resources at maximum speed, if as a result of this policy the stock is exhausted the sooner. Yet this has happened before, and may happen again. The world's mineral stocks, notably, are only theoretically inexhaustible. They appear endless when they are not. It is not advisable to use them up prodigally when we know that they are unreplaceable. Substitutes cannot always be found. The depletion of our natural stores is a piece of folly that no one will encourage, socialists least of all. To have a nation grow rapidly is a questionable advantage, since the law of decreasing returns obtains everywhere. It is possible to develop power and prestige at the expense of posterity. To skim from the top has been a temptation for many settlers of virgin lands with riches beckoning on all sides, but ere long the exploiting nation pays the penalty. Socialism, precisely because it sees far ahead, will discountenance ruthless exploitation and will husband our resources.

A gain in natural resources is therefore not well possible. If income is to be raised it will be by changes in labor supply and its efficiency.

§ 3. **Effects of Age Distribution on Production.**— But before passing to a consideration of such changes in the amount of labor-power which socialism may bring about, let us see what important features of population socialism can*not* directly, nor perhaps indirectly, affect. It will teach us to appreciate the uncontrollable factor in population, while otherwise we might exaggerate the powers of socialism.

Different populations show very different distributions of age, and this is important because not all ages are equally productive. Rather, we may divide life into several periods according to their economic productiveness. The first ten years, e. g., represent a clear loss, for at this time the child consumes without producing anything. In the second period, say from the tenth to the twentieth year, it begins to produce, but less than it consumes. There are of course exceptions, and besides it is difficult to rate productivity as soon as we refer to values-in-exchange. But roughly a balance between income and outgo, between what is produced and what is consumed, may be struck. Let us then call the third period from twenty to sixty or seventy years the most valuable for the nation. In these years the average man produces more than he consumes, and certainly much more than the biologically necessary things. He raises his income by raising his productiveness. It is the time of rearing children and laying aside savings for a rainy day. Production somewhere between thirty and sixty years of age is at topnotch. After the sixtieth or seventieth year we note a

TABLE TWO

AGE DISTRIBUTION IN THE POPULATION OF DIFFERENT COUNTRIES IN 1910

(Distribution in Percentages of the Total Population)

Countries

Age Periods	U. S. A.	France	Germany	Austria	Australia	United Kingdom
1–10 Years	...22.2%	17.2%	23.1%	26.3%	41.1%	20.7%
10–20 Years	...19.8%	16.6%	20.3%	20 %		19 %
20–30 Years	...18.7%	15.9%	16.3%	15.4%	32 %	8.9%
30–40 Years	...14.6%	14.8%	15.2%	12.6%		16.1%
40–50 Years	...10.6%	12.6%	10.2%	10.5%	18.8%	13.3%
50–60 Years	... 7.2%	10.5%	7.7%	7.7%		9.7%
Over Sixty Years	.... 6.9%	12.4%	7.2%	7.5%	7.7%	6.4%
Total Population in Millions	...92	39.2	65	28.5	4.45	45.4

Note: Age-Periods for the United Kingdom are the following: One to Ten Years; Ten to Twenty Years; Twenty to Twenty-Five Years; Twenty-Five to Thirty-Five Years; Thirty-Five to Forty-Five Years; Forty-Five to Fifty-Five Years; Fifty-Five to Sixty-Five Years; Over Sixty-Five Years.

Reference: Statistical Yearbooks of United States, France, Germany, Austria, Australia, United Kingdom.

decline. The curve of productiveness falls visibly. Man once more becomes a deficit producer and eventually depends entirely upon others for his living. But consumption of course drops off also.

Now Table Two is designed to show some striking differences between such powers as the United States and Germany, and smaller nations like France or Austria on the other hand. The size of the population is not however the point in question. Rather, it is the effect of *net birth-rates and of migration.* It will be noted that the first two nations mentioned boast a large percentage of young ages, while their proportion of advanced ages is relatively small. In the United States immigration was always a dominant factor. In Germany the natural increase counts most up to 1900, and after that decreasingly so, while immigration increases. The period of twenty to forty years is well represented in both countries. Labor is cheap relative to resources, and there's enough to make rapid internal development possible. Powers grow great and rich when the demographic pyramid bulges at the bottom and is contracted at the top, for then the surplus producers or, from a given time standpoint, the prospective surplus producers provide an ample investment fund. The condition of France and Austria is serious. France suffered most through a decline of the birth-rate; Austria through emigration. Her best men left in the prime of manhood. No nation can easily offset such a drain.

There is no need of developing further this point. The differences of age distribution are sufficiently wellknown, but they are recalled here as significant by comparison with such changes in the labor-supply as socialism may at will bring about. The factors not so controllable influence the supply at least as much, and possibly more.

§ 4. **Possible Increase of the Labor Supply.**— The possibilities of socialistic readjustment are tabulated in Table Three. The estimate is of course only a rough one, for statistics are not always on a strictly comparative basis. There is plenty of room for error. Classifications do not correspond exactly, and the statistical service is not for all countries equally reliable and complete. But so far as the numerical changes in the labor supply are concerned the appended table is suggestive. It shows

TABLE THREE

Possible Changes in the Labor Supply of the United States for the Year 1910, according to Socialistic Standards

(References: Thirteenth Census of the United States, Census Bureau, Volumes on Population and on Occupations.)

A. NUMBER OF GAINFULLY OCCUPIED AND NON-OCCUPIED IN 1910
(Millions omitted)

Total population			92
Gainfully occupied		38.2	
Not gainfully occupied		53.8	
Of these were:			
Married women	16.1	after deduction of gainfully occupied.	
Children under 20 years	31.2		
Females over 65 years	2.1		
Males over 70 years	1.1		
Youths attending school over 20 years of age	0.6		
Widows under 65 years	1.6		
Inmates of benevolent institutions	0.6		
Inmates of prisons	0.1		
Idle rich, etc.	0.4		

B. CHANGES IN LABOR SUPPLY CONFORMING TO SOCIALISTIC STANDARDS

(Millions omitted)

Losses		*Gains*	
1. Abolition of work for children under 20. (Count their efficiency at one-half)	3.7	1. Industrial employment of married women under 60 years of age. (Count their present efficiency as two-thirds that developed under socialism)	4.8
2. Pensions for all over 60. (Count four-fifths of all males, and one-half of females over 60 as gainfully occupied in 1910).	4.1	2. Employment of all between 20 and 60 years of age not gainfully occupied in 1910 (excepting disabled, etc.)	2.1

Losses		*Gains*	
		3. Reduction of involuntary unemployment, except through illness	0.6
Gross loss	7.8	Gross gain	7.5
In per cent. of gainfully occupied	20.4%	In per cent. of gainfully occupied	19.6%
3. Loss through reduction of work hours per week	20 %	4. Gain through educational extension, etc., say	25 %
Total gross loss in percentages	40.4%	Total gross gain	44.6%
		Deducting gross loss	40.4%
		Net gain	4.2%
		Allow for errors, giving socialism the benefit of the doubt	10 %
		Final net gain possible	14.2%

that more than a ten or fifteen per cent. gain, even when we speculate on the effects of education, should not be expected by socialists. The losses incident to the introduction of socialistic ideals almost counterbalance the gains.

If we figure the possible gains and losses for the United States on the basis of occupation statistics for 1910 the account would run about as follows.

The population of the United States in 1910 was ninety-two million. Of these slightly over thirty-eight million were gainfully occupied. That is, they supported themselves entirely or mainly by their own earnings, the remainder of the population depending upon them for a living. The majority thus was not gainfully occupied officially, though many of them doubtless helped to produce values sold in the open market. In addition, we note, there were nearly eighteen million married women exclusively of those gainfully occupied, plus the following non-producers who earned neither money nor otherwise contributed directly to the nation's fund of utilities. Namely, we have first all children under twenty years of age, of whom there were thirty million; secondly the aged who account for three million, third, young men and women attending educational institutions, fourth, widows not gainfully occupied but less than sixty-five years of age, and finally such other groups as criminals, cripples, and the idle rich. The classification will point out which of these several classes are available for industrial employment, and which are not.

Socialism hopes to gain most by industrializing the work of women. The abolition of the home is understood by most socialists in this sense. It is not that they wish to break up the personal relation between the married and their offspring, but that they advocate the consolidation of homes into larger units of social life, or if not that, the conversion of individual work into team work so that unnecessary duplication and waste may be minimized. It is difficult to decide just what socialists propose to do, as current events in Russia show. But it seems best to grant socialists a gain of one-third by their new methods of utilizing female labor. The question of home ties and legal relations may then be ignored entirely. It will be noted however that the gain refers only to women not now industrially employed, and then only to those under sixty years of age.

This second restriction of age follows from the socialistic norm of leisure. An organic law of the Russian Socialist Federal Soviet Republic, e. g., has classified men over sixty and women over fifty years of age as unable to work. To these age groups it grants a pension, and expects no work except it be voluntarily done — which it doubtless often is. It seems not unreasonable to figure on a loss, therefore, in our calculation of all over sixty who are now gainfully occupied or working as wives and mothers. If we count them as normally efficient this means a loss of over four million workers.

But to return to the sources of gain. There is in the second place, the employment under socialism of all between twenty and sixty years of age — on our supposition that pensions begin with the sixtieth year. No professional loafers will be tolerated. Wealth will be no excuse for idleness, and aversion to work no passport for tramps. A great many widows under sixty years of age that now live on their income will go to work, too; and perhaps some of those now attending school will not do so after socialism has improved the lower school system. The total gain thus will amount to over two million, as indicated in the Table.

But this is not all. In the third place unemployment may be materially reduced. In 1910 about one-half million men and women were out of work throughout the year. In some years the loss is still greater, in others much smaller. It is a debatable point indeed whether socialism will improve the productive organization enough to eliminate all this waste. Not many will agree that it can be done. But in order to make the argument as strong as possible we may for the moment grant the adjustment of supply to demand in goods and labor that socialists demand. An improvement is certainly desirable, and, what is more to the point, seems practicable.

This leaves us, in the fourth place, a gain due to education. In allowing for this change we are passing from purely quantitative to qualitative aspects of the labor-supply. It is not certain that any kind of estimate is worth while, since efficiency depends on so much else besides technical training. But as a rule an advancement of learning must be held to have perceptible effects. The gain should be real, and in excess of what prevailing conditions will lead to. Hence a 25% addition to the gains already registered is proposed in the Table.

If now we turn to the loss we have first the effect of protection for old age, which was referred to above, and secondly the shrinkage of labor-power due to a prohibition of child labor. One of the most fundamental assets of the socialistic doctrine is its educational program. Knowledge is to be popularized and made free. The average man will have a chance to learn and think as he has not had heretofore. Technical instruction and a liberal education in the arts and social inquiries will develop the mind, while recreation and hygiene will develop the body. Without education leisure means little, and without leisure education is impossible. The abolition of child labor has thus several motives. It looks to the intellectual uplift of the masses, and it aims at health and vigor. The dissemination of knowledge is only to be accompanied by a greater regard for physical welfare.

Just at what age industrial employment is to begin we cannot tell. It has been urged that all youths should have a college education, in which case the period of leisure would have to be extended to the twenty-second year. Others have been content to stop at fifteen. But in as much as the present common school education is found so woefully wanting by all parties, even though it includes eight years of training, it seems proper to credit the socialistic scheme with an extension of schooling at least up to the twentieth year. The less it approaches this goal the weaker its argument, and the smaller of course the gain in productiveness which we have already put on the right side of the ledger.

If then we combine these two reductions in labor supply we have a total of seven million eight hundred thousand, against which must be set a gain of seven million five hundred thousand. This leaves a net preliminary loss of three hundred thousand workers. However, the gain in efficiency, which was rated at 25%, more than counterbalances it. A loss of three hundred thousand workers equals not quite one per cent. of the total number of gainfully occupied who, it will be remembered, made up about thirty-eight million out of a total population of ninety-two million. Deduct this loss of 0.8% from a gain of 25% and you obtain an apparent net gain of 24.2%.

But the gain is apparent only. For in the third place socialism loses by curtailing the number of work-hours per day, week, and year. In 1918 the standard day had about eight hours. Yet many millions worked ten hours a day or over. In 1910 the eight hour schedule was still the exception rather than the rule. Under socialism it may be the rule at first, but the avowed intention of all socialists is the reduction of labor-hours proportionate to technical advance. The more machinery displaces the hand, and the greater the output of goods per hour or month, the shorter the work day. This is the slogan with which socialists fight. It is logical in a way, and should serve to benefit the carefree masses. But the loss counts and means a shrinkage of goods, that is, not an absolute shrinkage, but one relative to maximum possibilities, or to what is now being done. If we take an average weekly schedule of fifty hours, and clip off one-fifth, we lose in commodities what we gain in freedom. Socialism is willing apparently to reckon with six or seven hours of work a day, and so our deduction of 20% is fair.

We conclude then that nominally the gain in labor-power is less than 5%. However, as remarked, there is no need of sticking too closely to our figures, since there is so much chance for error. Let us, therefore, return to our first announced gain of ten to fifteen per cent., which would be a maximum compatible with the ideals of socialism. More than that it cannot look forward to without becoming untrue to its own professions.

§ 5. **Possible Economy in Technical Organization.**—There remain thus for brief consideration two other sets of facts, namely, first the continuance of disagreeable types of labor, and secondly certain savings due to organization such as socialism hopes to perfect.

Irksome and dirty work will always have to be done, for as fast as machines in one place relieve men of it, needs in another place reintroduce it. It is likely that in the future occupational diseases and accidents will almost entirely disappear. Science increasingly finds means for protecting the laborer against the poisons amidst which he plies his trade. Safety devices will be multiplied and employees properly taught the use of machines. Ignorance, carelessness, and fatigue have been found to be the most common sources of fatal accidents. Socialism is no doubt right if it claims that the perils of work can be largely eliminated by right precautionary measures. But this is not doing away with crude labor as such.

Disagreeable labor will always have to be done because man's wants are never completely satisfied. There's always something to attend to, to invent and to produce. As fast as men are displaced by one machine they find employment in some other quarter. Crude labor means energy, and a certain amount of human muscular energy is an indispensable part of the productive organization. The ratio between rough work and the more refined, between manual labor and machino-facture, technical progress cannot materially change. In the Census figures for 1910 crude labor is just about as prominent numerically as twenty or thirty years earlier. There is no perceptible decline of unskilled occupations or of hard work in the building trades, in engineering, mining and farming. Machines liberate labor for less essential uses, but they do not end cheerless toil. If socialism then

TABLE FOUR

Industries With Small-Scale Production (U. S., 1910)

Industries	Per cent. of Wage-Earners in Establishments Employing No Wage-Earners, or Less than Twenty (20)
Bakery products	75%
Butter, cheese, and milk	80%
Canning and preserving	31%
Carriage and wagons	40%
Cooperage	31%
Flour mill products	82%
Unspecified food preparations	40%
Fur goods	57%
Manufactured ice	65%
Leather goods	32%
Marble works	34%
Mattresses and beds	43%
Mineral and soda waters	99%
Cottonseed oil	34%
Patent medicines	62%
Printing	58%
Tobacco manufactures	52%
Carved wood	45%

Reference: Thirteenth Census, 1910, V. 8, Manufactures, P. 186, U. S. Bureau of Census.

wishes to relieve the masses in this respect, it will have to alternate types of work for given individuals, or else take the sting out of the most dreaded kinds of labor by paying extra wages.

This would of course mean some impairment of social efficiency, but it might be worth while nonetheless. Besides, there is some room for economy in another field, namely in the organization of capital and labor forces. Socialists commonly dwell on this possibility and point to the immense loss now incurred by the public due to overproduction, to unnecessary duplication of plant, small-scale output, and extravagance in the use of machinery as well as of consumption goods.

The first kind of waste is of course attributed to the lack of correlation between demand and supply, and is therefore a distributive problem which connects closely with the problem of income, of which more hereafter.

Waste through useless duplication of effort and wealth results naturally from the individualistic principle and cannot be altogether avoided until the entire nation is treated as one market for one single producer, the government acting on behalf of the people. At the present an enterpriser is chiefly influenced by personal considerations. He will be willing to invest funds if they promise returns, even though the waste for the consuming public is perfectly apparent. Railroads, telephones, street car lines, ships and pikes, factories and office buildings have been needlessly duplicated in this manner. The waste occasionally has raised a storm of protest, but usually the charge upon the consumer has been borne with equanimity, as a sort of toll levied by Dame Liberty.

Socialism proposes to substitute a collectivistic principle for the competitive, and thus to end the drain on national resources that selfish duplication entails. It hopes to effect a noticeable saving by a better disposition of labor forces, and it seems reasonable to grant it all the credit that such a change may give the consumer.

The policy of consolidation, however, not merely leads

to a reduction of waste, it also is believed by some to lower costs on the principle that rates of return rise with increase of the scale of production.

In the United States in 1910 there were still a good many industries in which the number of employees per plant was less than twenty. Indeed, in many of them it was less than ten. Table Four shows typical instances of such small scale production. Three quarters of the bakeries, it will be seen, employed less than twenty workers. In the soda water production the percentage is highest, and creameries come next. Goods in these industries may be said to be produced on a small scale, but whether this means waste is another question. It is probable that the manufacturer has adjusted himself to the competitive conditions surrounding him and either cannot extend his business greatly, or else is tending in that direction without our noticing it at once. A bakery, for instance, is no longer a one-man affair. Machines have largely displaced manual labor. Some concerns supply many thousands of customers each day. The man who once had only one or two apprentices now employs ten or fifteen, installing machinery which gives him the largest return in profits. He has enlarged his scale of production, but it seems small compared to the methods used in iron and steel, or in mining.

The general answer is, however, the old one. Namely, fine work will always be in demand. There are crafts that call for high personal skill, individuality, and extreme care in workmanship. For such products large-scale production is out of the question. Their existence is simply evidence of wealth and high prices paid for special quality. Socialism will make an end, possibly, of some of these industries, but this gain of labor-power for uses elsewhere is a detail.

On the other hand, if scrapping of machinery and of labor which now is carried on extravagantly can be stopped by collectivistic norms of valuation, a notable saving will be effected. It has been freely admitted by magnates of business that the competitive struggle involves a large waste through rapid obsolescence of capital goods. A slight improvement may lead to the abandonment of an old process and of the tools going with it. The fear of a competitor who may himself introduce improvements at any cost to win the market is a factor deciding the issue. It is not the cheapening of production that counts, but the difference in sales resulting from any degree of cheapening. If the machine means only a five per cent. saving in "socially necessary labor," to use Marx's expression, the old machine will not be scrapped on socialistic principles. But if between competitors a five per cent. cost reduction means the difference of holding or losing a market the new machine will be installed regardless of what society loses by the substitution. Capitalism not only tolerates but encourages fads and fashions, the discarding of the old, and the frequent renewal of both production and consumption goods. It is not for most people a question of wearing out apparel, but of being in style. The adventitious values of fashion and elegance which human nature makes possible and social organization has assiduously cultivated for ulterior motives, these values move us to spend our money when we know we shouldn't. Utility is no longer primary, but secondary. We wear clothes not to be warm and comfortable, but to look well or at any rate look up to date. Waste is not illogically taken to be circumstantial evidence of wealth. We may fool our good friends and really have less than they are led to believe, but the impression we make repays us for our reckless outlays.

Socialism may put a curb to this sort of display and waste. Of course, it would be hard to decide whether, for one thing, it can be done, and for another thing, whether the saving would mount up sufficiently, but it is well to grant socialism a gain of labor-power on this score.

§ 6. Possible Recomposition of the National Income. — Savings of this kind however bring us to the second means of a general character for raising the incomes of the masses. The first, we noted, was an increase of labor, natural resources, or of efficiency tested per individual or socially. By these methods we have found an increase of ten or fifteen per cent. in wages to be made possible. But since this is not enough a change in the *composition* of the national output of goods will have to accompany a change in volume. If we can get rid of all useless types of labor which do not cater to the average wage earner, and convert this energy into more generally useful services, then the gain will be real, even though a few rich people are hard hit.

The extent of this change in the ratio of necessities and luxuries may be gauged in several ways. We may consult first, the distribution of income, secondly the statistics on manufactures in which many of the luxuries appear, and thirdly the occupation statistics in which may be found most of the services figuring in large incomes.

Table Five will serve to indicate the main facts of distribution for 1910. It will be noticed that it is quite unequal, the great majority having less than $1000 a year, while a few boast an income of several millions. Forty per cent of all the families in the United States had less than $700 annually, seven-tenths had not over $1000, and only about ten per cent. had in excess of $1500. Yet the national income at that time was about

$32,000,000,000, of which probably some twenty-five billion represented consumable goods for personal use. The remainder consisted of capital goods. If then we divide this smaller sum of $25,000,000,000 by a popula-

TABLE FIVE

The Distribution of Incomes in the United States in 1910

(Estimates of Dr. W. I. King, in his "Wealth and Income of the People of the United States," pages 224–228.)

Family Income of not over	Cumulative Number of Income-receiving Units, in Thousands	Cumulative Amount of Income, in Millions of Dollars
$700	10,878	5,807
$1,000	19,402	12,969
$1,200	22,830	16,703
$1,500	25,243	19,867
$2,400	27,016	23,158
$4,000	27,496	24,660
$5,200	27,644	25,326
$10,000	27,818	26,514
$100,000	27,941.6	29,521
$1,000,000	27,945	30,038
Grand Total	27,945.2	30,529

THE DISTRIBUTION IN PERCENTAGES

Family Income of not over	Cumulative Percentage of Families Having Given Income	Cumulative Percentage of Total Income Received by Given Class of Families
$700	38.92%	19.02%
$1,000	69.43%	42.48%
$1,500	90.31%	65.08%
$2,400	96.18%	74.71%

tion of ninety-two million we obtain a per capita income of approximately $270. Multiply this by five, and the average family would have an income of $1350. This might, according to socialistic standards, be called the normal income at that date. The standard of living is not fixed rigidly any more by socialists than by economists. It varies with time and place, and above all it varies with the productiveness of the nation. There is an objective standard set by the requirements of physical and mental vigor, and a subjective one kept in mind by the individual. Socialism may consider that income normal which at any time embraces the largest class of consumers. In that case $1000 annually would be more nearly the goal to steer for than $1350. But it is certain that socialists aim at a marked improvement of the general mode of living. Their ambitions are well known. The quantitative aspect of this desire for betterment will doubtless involve a thorough revision of family budgets. A reapportioning of goods and services will take place, so that all families have the luxuries now (1910) enjoyed by those with $1500 a year or more.

Four-fifths of the American people in 1910 had not over $1200 income. Luxuries for them were but a small part of their budget. It is indeed doubtful whether at the purchasing power of money for 1910 a family with a hundred dollars a month could have spent more than five per cent. on luxuries. But the other fifth of the population had so much the more. The great bulk of its expenses consisted, according to our definition of a standard of living at that time, of luxuries. Thus, if we make due allowance for what the rich spend in the purchase of necessities, we have about one-fifth of the national income represented by luxuries. It is this fifth which socialism will turn over to the poor. Or rather it is the labor and capital required for producing these luxuries that socialism will turn into other channels. The output of necessities and comforts will increase, and that of extreme luxuries will end.

The statistics on manufactures throw further light on the matter. They do not, to be sure, contain all of the luxuries consumed by the wealthy. A variety of things for the use of which the rich are noted is not enumerated by the census taker. There are magnificent mansions, for instance, and golf links and racing stables and Pekingese dogs, and rare viands and art works and pleasure yachts and private Pullmans, and display-fountains and liveried servants and curios and opera seats, fancy dress balls and silver plate, and tiaras and mausoleums, none of which will be found in the official records. Yet they figure in the budgets of the plutocrats.

Again, it is impossible to tell from the official classification whether an article is really a luxury or not. The output of woolen mills, for instance, may be luxury or necessity according to quality of the fabric. The choice of tailor and of trimmings will further guide us in defining the finished suit. It may either prove to be a high-class luxury or if the material was made up in the sweatshop, we may be able to buy the suit at such a low figure that we refuse to class it among the luxuries. Shape and style, finish and quality of ingredient, time and place of purchase, these and other items decide whether the commodity is a necessity or not.

But even if the limitations of a statistical compilation are glaring, the appended Table Six will have some usefulness. Whether we agree on all the articles or not, the omitted items will probably somewhere near balance those listed wrongly. Within ten or fifteen per cent. the list of manufactured luxuries will agree with facts. With this understanding it is instructive to note that 10.4% of the aggregate of manufactures consisted of luxuries, the production of which required 11.2% of the total labor-force, entrepreneurs and superintendents, etc., included. These figures apply to the year 1914 when the total national income was about thirty-five billion dollars. In terms of that total, therefore, the luxuries amounted to 7%, while the producing forces made up about 2.5% of all gainfully occupied in that year.

Most of this material and energy can no doubt be turned to better uses. Socialism has a large field to cultivate, and great are the possibilities for reform by way of a recomposition of our national budget.

It is possible, e. g., to build cottages with the product of brickyards and quarries that now help to build palaces and accessory edifices on the estates of the multi-millionaire. It might even be possible to furnish every family a decent apartment to live in, or a house and lot such as the middle classes now point to with pride! In 1910 there were over twenty million families in the United States, of which nearly eleven million rented their homes. It is difficult to get at the number of houses occupied by one family or a single tenant because the Census Bureau classed every sort of sleeping quarters as a dwelling, while conversely every dwelling place figured as one family.[2] Thus a single occupant of a tent or way-car or boathouse was rated as a family, but so were all the inmates of a hotel. They too were counted as *one* family. Owing to such irresponsible procedure in classification there is no direct way for finding out how many families had an individual home of their own. However, it is significant that only nine million out of twenty million families owned the place they lived in. Judging from that circumstance we can hardly count on more than one dwelling house for every two families in the country. And

[2] "Thirteenth Census of U. S.," Census Bureau, Volume 1, p. 1285.

TABLE SIX

American Manufactures in 1914 Which Were Consumed Chiefly by People Earning Over $1200 a Year

(Reference: U. S. Census Bureau, Manufactures in 1914.)
(Thousands omitted)

Industry	Number of Persons Engaged in Industry	Value of Product $
Artificial flowers	9,300	19,000
Artists' materials	1,000	3,000
Automobile and parts	146,000	633,000
Fancy boxes	50,600	75,000
Carpets not rag carpets	33,000	69,000
Chocolate	5,000	36,000
Clocks and watches	25,000	34,000
Fancy articles, not elsewhere specified	13,300	25,000
Fireworks	1,500	2,300
Fur goods	15,200	46,400
Leather gloves	12,300	21,600
Haircloth and hairwork	2,300	5,700
Jewelry	46,000	119,000
Millinery and lace	54,000	114,000
Mineral waters	25,000	58,000
Motorcycles	7,700	22,000
Musical instruments	55,000	120,000
Fountain pens	2,200	7,500
Photographic apparatus	11,300	39,000
Rubber goods, not elsewhere specified	62,000	224,000
Silk goods	116,000	254,000
Silverware	18,400	38,200
Sporting goods	6,300	13,000
Stationery, not elsewhere specified	9,000	22,000
Stationery and art goods	2,400	4,000
Toys and games	9,000	14,000
Upholstering materials	5,000	16,000
Washing machines	3,000	7,600
Carved woods	13,400	19,000
Woolen goods	170,000	395,000
Total here listed	930,000	2,516,000
Absolute total	8,265,000	24,200,000
Percentage of listed workers and values	11.2%	10.4%

of these many live in crowded quarters, a few rooms to the family with small regard for sanitation.

Considering all things it seems therefore best not to expect too much at once from a regrouping of concrete commodities entering into the average family budget. But there is more chance for doing away with useless types of labor such as now cater mainly to the wealthy. The producers of intangible goods, that is of personal services, are all too numerous from the standpoint of the small earner. Much energy might be liberated by shifting these producers to new fields, by rearranging the ratios of different kinds of personal service now rendered. On socialist principles this change should certainly be strongly urged.

Table Seven gives the main facts relating to this question. It will be seen that in 1910 nearly two-fifths of the people gainfully occupied were not producing concrete goods, the majority figuring under the professions or as traders, domestic servants. Out of a total of 38,000,000 the professional group — teachers, lawyers, etc. — accounts for nearly 5%, the domestic and personal services for more than 12%, and the personnel employed in transportation and trade for another 20%. These are the workers that did not produce food or clothing, but consumed both in rendering a different sort of value. Some of them of course were indispensable to the methods of production and to the scale of production which made food and clothing so plentiful. It would be folly to consider the employment of all of them as unnecessary to the production of tangible goods. Socialism does not assert this, nor will any one expect socialism to abolish such services altogether.

The chief task is a reduction of this number, so that the army of farmers and manufacturers is increased. In

TABLE SEVEN

Number of Gainfully Occupied in the United States in 1910, to be Reduced or Eliminated Under Socialism

(Reference: United States Census on Occupations for 1910.)

A. THE GAINFULLY OCCUPIED IN SPECIFIED SERVICES
(Thousands omitted)

Engaged in Transportation	2,637	
Trade	3,615	
Public services	459	
Professional services	1,664	
Domestic and personal services	3,772	
Clerical occupations	1,737	
Total	13,884	

Note: This represents labor not engaged directly in the Production of *concrete* goods.

B. ESTIMATED SAVINGS IN CERTAIN OCCUPATIONS
(Thousands omitted)

In Transportation

Carriage drivers	35
Chauffeurs	46
Garage keepers	5
Hostlers, etc.	63
Livery stables	35
Teamsters, etc.	16
Railroad employees	1,247
Express, telegraph, etc.	314
Others	322
Total	2,083
Estimate saving at ⅓	694

In Trade

Bankers	56
Brokers of all kinds	49
Store clerks, salespersons, etc.	1,368
Commercial travelers	164
Window-dressers, etc.	5
Deliverymen	230
Floor walkers, etc.	21
Samplers, etc.	13
Insurance agents	98
Porters, etc.	102
Newsboys	30
Employment office owners, elevators, etc.	22
Real estate agents	126
Retailers	1,195
Wholesalers	51
Canvassers, etc.	105
Book-keepers, etc.	487
Other clerks	720
Total	4,842
Estimate saving at ⅔	3,226

In Public Services

Marshals, sheriffs, etc.	24
Policemen	64
Soldiers, sailors	77
Total	163
Estimate saving at ⅓	55

In Professional Services

Lawyers, etc.	115
Notaries	7
Keepers of charitable institutions, etc.	23
Total	145
Estimate saving at ⅔	100

In Personal and Domestic Services

Barbers, etc.	195
Bartenders and barkeepers	231
Elevator boys, etc.	25
Janitors and sextons	113
Hotelkeepers, etc.	65
Housekeepers (lodging, etc.)	189
Laborers, unspecified	53
Personal servants	1,572
Waiters, etc.	188
Total	2,631
Estimate saving at ¾	2,000
Total saving	6,075
All gainfully occupied in 1910	38,200
Per cent. of saving	15.9%

1910 about three-fifths of the population furnished all the commodities. Whatever the entire population needed, that was produced by 62% of it. No more eloquent testimony to the wealth of the United States and to the efficiency of its people could be given. It is the result of the same conditions that made it possible for twelve million farmers and farm-laborers to feed the remaining eighty-five million, besides having something left for exportation. A rich country will naturally add many personal services to its fund of concrete consumables. The trend toward non-necessities is thus illustrated, and no one would wish a return to the costlier system of the "simple life."

Yet it is plain that a notable portion of this intangible wealth benefits only a very few, and that much of it is either quite useless, or outright injurious and demoralizing for the general run of people. It is not well that so much energy is wasted in the rendering of trivial services. Hundreds of thousands of domestic servants are not needed, especially among those who employ them in large numbers. Neither will socialism have much use for the millions that now are engaged in commerce or in some of the professions. We find in the list, for instance, commercial travelers and book agents, floor walkers and private secretaries, clerks and typists, teamsters and messenger boys, advertising agents and curb brokers, printers and journalists, janitors and watchmen, body guards and doorkeepers, manicures and maids-in-waiting, charity workers and chauffeurs for private families. A certain percentage of these will and should be retained, but many of them socialism will place in other positions. If, as suggested in the Table, we select certain occupations and then decide upon a curtailment according to the nature of the services now rendered, we shall find that somewhere about one-half of the total number of gainfully occupied *not* producing concrete goods may be cut off. About 16% of *all* gainfully occupied in 1910 would thus go into new lines of work.

It should be noted in passing that our three tests of luxury consumption and therefore of the possibility for a rise of the average man's income correspond roughly. In each case we find a difference of about one-fifth. The redistribution of this fifth marks the extent to which socialism is tolerably sure of helping the masses who in 1910 earned less than $1000 or $1200 per year.

§ 7. **Other Limits in Production.**— Whether all of the poor would hail the readjustment with delight, however, is a question, for the change will involve some losses as well as a great gain. It is ever so. The well-to-do, of course, will suffer most, since the recomposition of the national budget also means a redistribution of incomes. To them the elimination of luxuries in goods and services will bring the greatest sacrifices. But it will also have a drawback for the masses of the people who have long been used to the glamor of city life as competitive principles engendered it. There are some features about the present method of retailing goods that those who bother not about maximum welfare will prefer to the socialistic scheme. And one cannot altogether blame them.

The possession of concrete goods is not everything even to those of limited means. There is some satisfaction in seeing what one cannot own, and there are many who prefer the courtesies of a competitive business to the precision of a public service controlled by the state. Thus some will feel that little is gained by having an extra pair of shoes or twice the allowance in furniture, if the goods must be bought from a government-owned warehouse where the clerk cares nothing about the customer, but on the contrary is conscious of rights which place him at an advantage. Shopping is now made a pleasure by those who wish to attract patrons and expand business regardless of social welfare, or perhaps in full harmony with it. The down-town districts of a large city are a commentary on the spirit of modern enterprises. Everything is subordinated to the maxim for profits. The customer is always right — as long as he pays the price. Many people enjoy this situation and would rather have the window displays of a fashionable department store than cheaper ribbon or better housing conditions. And so with the services of newsboy and shoeblack and hotel-porter and all the rest of servitors catering to the rich chiefly, but to the poor also in some measure.

And lastly, it is likely that the law of diminishing returns will set limits to the output of comforts regardless of what socialism decrees or the people may desire. The staples of life are most subject to decrease in accordance with the principle first enunciated by the Ricardians. We cannot add to our agricultural stores at random as we may increase the output of minerals. These latter returns need not fall off for long times to come, but in so far as farm-products furnish the basis for manufacturing, or supply the population with foods, the national labor-power is always at its mercy. Thus in European countries the peak of productivity has long been reached. In the United States, whatever increases in acre-yield may come, will be expensive. The farmer is sure to sell at a rising price. The gain will be smaller than the cost in labor and capital. The yield per acre may rise, but expenses will rise even more. The more luxuries of one kind the socialist demands, the more of another kind he will have to forego, or else do without a corresponding amount of necessaries.

The nineteenth century established many records that will not be repeated for a long while. Thanks to them the white race has multiplied its income in goods, learning to cherish precisely such ideals of future development as socialism stands for. But it is not likely that the next few hundred years will witness a similar growth in tillable acreage, in timber supply, and in the output of minerals. Science and organization have done their utmost. They have made the nineteenth century the wonder of all ages. Yet the level of living has for the masses not risen as much as socialists expect to raise it hereafter, nor has the flow of luxuries sufficed to satisfy the masses. In Europe foreign trade proved a valuable means for the diversification of living. The output of factory and mine was exchanged for raw materials bought abroad, and the teeming millions were fed with stocks grown in the Americas or in the plains of Siberia and Australia. Even the East Indies and the dark continent furnished a quota.

This, then, is the secret of a high level of living among the minority of Europeans. By exporting large values in tiny packages they managed to obtain the basic materials or rare luxuries. In the future, however, this will not be so easy. The more densely populated the erstwhile frontier lands, that were the granaries of Europe, the less certain their exports of foods, and more self sufficient the European nations must become. The regulation of the birthrate is one means of frustrating the designs of a sinister law of nature, but this is not a peculiarly socialistic means. Nor do wars solve the problem. The war just closed e. g., has slain many millions, but it has also exterminated the ablest instead of the worst, and that reacts disadvantageously upon both agriculture and industry. The only alternative to a reduced food allowance, consequently, is an increased acre yield at the cost of comforts and luxuries. In the long run nobody can escape this situation.

People in the United States do not entertain such fears of a reduction in food. Yet there are indications that for them, too, future gains will mean a more than proportionate expense of human and mechanical energy. True, if the United Kingdom can produce thirty-five bushels of wheat per acre, so can we. But this is nothing to gloat over. On the contrary we should regret the step. Furthermore, it will particularly interfere with socialistic plans, since the workers set free by the elimination of useless services will increasingly be drawn to the farm instead of producing manufactures.

Within a few generations such a turn for the worse is certain unless, as remarked before, birth-control is popularized as one may expect it will be. But in any case it deserves notice that in the distant future the over-populated countries will not be able to fall back upon machinofactures for a supply of necessities. The world is becoming rapidly settled. Frontier regions still exist, but may not have foodstuffs to export in such amounts as the nineteenth century Europe needed. When that date arrives socialism will have only one refuge for the poorly endowed countries. Namely, it will have to fund the world's supplies so as to maintain a high level of living among the least favored nations. The increase of luxuries may then continue, but it will not reach the proportions some hope for, and the funding process which is after all the logical goal of economic socialism will encroach further upon the luxury rations of the inhabitants in the richest lands. Thus will production have found its limits.

CHAPTER VII

THE LIMITS IN DISTRIBUTION

§ 1. The Spending Power of the Rich.— Production determines distribution. A nation cannot distribute more among its members than it has at its disposal per annum in goods and services. To the extent, therefore, that socialism fails in augmenting the social dividend it must also fail in raising the level of living of the average man. This is on the understanding that the total national income is divided evenly between all the citizens. But of course, this equality never existed and is not contemplated by socialism.

There is consequently much room for a change of individual or family incomes without altering materially the productiveness of the nation. In 1910 two-fifths of the earning population received less than one-fifth of the national income, and one-fifth of the people claimed over one-half of the aggregate. To-day the distribution cannot be greatly different, though as a result of the war just brought to a conclusion some groups of labor have raised their purchasing power slightly, while some of the formerly well-to-do have lost heavily. Wars always mean a redistribution of incomes.

But the general fact is the same for all nations. We shall perhaps always have the poor with us if no radical change in economic organization takes place. The poor always have been in the majority so far, and because of this disparity existing everywhere the task of socialism is clearly defined. It may try, and it solemnly promises, to redistribute goods so that all have the necessities, and none spend greatly in excess of what the average man is allowed.

It should, however, be understood that the present unequal distribution is no worse than it has been in the past, that the largest incomes do not measure spending power, and that without state aid a slow diffusion of national wealth among all the inhabitants does take place. Socialistic literature has been somewhat misleading on these points.

The poor are to-day no worse off than they were in olden times. On the contrary, there is plenty of evidence to show that unmitigated pauperism is on the wane. Among the ancients wealth was unevenly distributed because land was the chief natural resource, and this belonged to a few. When the level of living comprised not much more than food and clothing even for the rich, then the chief privilege of the wealthy was leisure and power over the body. Slavery with all its attendant rights of the owner furnished a sense of power such as nowadays undoubtedly comes with the control of large industrial plants or public undertakings. All through the Middle Ages this division of privileges and duties was continued. The Church did not discourage it, though it preached now and then of the brotherhood of man. The line of division between lord and vassal, between freeman and serf, between noble and burgher was distinctly drawn and observed in social intercourse. The minority of nobles and clergy owned the land or held it in fee simple from the Crown or Holy See respectively, while the bulk of the population owned no more than the food they ate and the clothes on their back. It was not till the end of the fourteenth century that private ownership among the unnoble became important. Fortunes then were amassed with which eventually the middle class made itself master of political affairs. But the concentration of wealth was continued as before, except that new forms of wealth appeared, and that hereditary rights to office were overshadowed by inheritance of wealth. When this change came capitalism had won the day for the plebeian majority, even though income itself still fell into the hands of a small group of enterprisers.

Until quite recent times wealth was less powerful and conspicuous also in the sense that it could not buy what the rich now display so lavishly. The basis of national subsistence was agriculture. Manufactures made up the smallest part of the social dividend, so that income was spent mainly in the building of castles, and in viands and costly raiments. The materials were expensive enough, but the total effect of such extravagances was not as obvious as it is to-day. Palaces were for protection rather than for comfort, or if meant for comfort the limitations, at any rate, of the value of money were much more apparent than to-day. Science had not yet made the discoveries that furnished the immense variety of comforts now so highly prized. The rich had more candles to burn, but the light was about the same. They had wood in the winter, but so had most of the tenants on the estate. Rich food and gorgeous though ill fitting apparel, security against the enemy in early ages such as the poor could not get, an abundance of silver and gold plate, and perhaps precious jewels from the Orient — such were the means by which the millionaires formerly made themselves envied. The forms of display were not as ostentatious as to-day, and the people were not as close to them. The chase and the feud were pastimes the multitude did not care for anyway. A difference in learning either did not exist or did not challenge attention because of the limits of science. And besides, the multitude until a few generations ago did not aspire to a status such as now is deemed the proof of well-being and democracy.

Again, however, it would be a mistake to assume that the excessively wealthy can spend all they have. The notion that a million dollar income is actually spent for comforts and luxuries, or might be so spent, is erroneous. It has already been shown in a previous chapter that the statistical data disprove such a contention. They show plainly that not over one-fifth of our national product consists of the non-necessities, and that more than one-half of this takes the shape of goods consumed almost entirely by incomes ranging between $1000 and $2500 for 1910, in the United States. Attention has been called also to the fact that a large portion of every nation's income represents capital goods used for producing concrete or inconcrete consumption goods. Hence this part of the total is not available for consumption. But it is owned mainly by the rich. The small earners save rarely more than one-fifth or tenth of their income. They cannot or will not do so. But the corporation making a 25% net profit, the man with a hundred thousand dollar income, these are the centers of financial power. From them the replacement and investment fund flows. They maintain the status quo of industry or expand business so as to raise the next year's social dividend. Out of the millionaire's income thus all but a minor fraction remains normally in productive condition. If all incomes over five thousand a year were to be spent in the purchase of luxuries, as has occasionally been suggested, our economic system would collapse. There would be no labor and capital to provide the necessities; nor could the plan for the rich men work out well. Such spending would prove to be impossible.

Large incomes then do not mean the scale of living that many associate with them. Nor should it be forgotten that nearly all wealth eventually redounds to the advantage of the masses. There is no discovery made by science, no invention patented by the manufacturer, no improvement introduced in the realm of exchange, but it sooner or later benefits the average man. It is not possible to secrete ideas forever. It is impossible to withhold permanently from the people the advantages first enjoyed by the wealthy. Most luxuries some day become necessities. Novelties in the course of time become antiquities and curiosities of science, commonplaces. A watch to-day is bought for a few dollars, though the work of many great men was necessary to produce it. A Galileo had to formulate laws of motion before we could measure time accurately. The dial contains figures that somebody many thousands of years ago invented. The processes for refining the ore used in the case cover many achievements scientific and mechanic. The purchaser of the watch does not pay for all he buys at the time. He, on the contrary, expects to get the benefit of ideas and efforts made by others, a few of them living, but most of them long dead. *Social heredity is the main source of unearned increments.* We profit by accepting the knowledge of our forebears. We all, in the long run, get the benefit of individual endeavor if it is extraordinary and of lasting value. The rich cannot corner the market of luxuries except for a short while.

Their own fortunes indeed crumble. From shirtsleeve to shirtsleeve is but three generations, according to an old adage. That does not seem to be true, and it certainly need not apply to the circulation of wealth. But it is true that many huge fortunes are dissipated soon after the founder has gone. In a hundred ways the hoard melts to nothing. Periodically some rich men become paupers, and some of the poor accumulate wealth.

Yet in general there is a permanent concentration of income. The disparity is lasting. The well-to-do continue to be so, and the wage earner of a thousand dollars or two per year continues to stay at that figure. From father to son we have wealth and poverty transmitted. This is the fact that socialism is conscious of and wishes to change. It wishes to hasten the natural diffusion of incomes which the laws of consumption bring about. It insists upon helping the laws of sociation here as at other points in the field of economic relations.

§ 2. Causes and Consequences of Concentration of Incomes.— Socialism has answered the question, why such gross inequalities of income exist, in the spirit of certain British writers whom Marx respected highly. The question of one and the reply of another will help to make clear the socialistic attitude, which from the days of Marx on has remained the same in this matter.

W. Thompson wrote in 1824: "How comes it that a nation abounding more than any other [he refers to England, of course] in the crude materials of wealth in machinery, dwellings and food, in intelligent and industrious producers, with all the apparent means of happiness, with all the outward semblance of happiness exhibited by a small and rich portion of the community, should pine still in privation? How comes it that the fruits of the labor of the industrious, after years of incessant and successful exertion, are mysteriously and without any imputation of fault to them, without any convulsion of nature swept away?" [1]

Conditions to-day are not as gloomy as those depicted

[1] Thompson, W., "Inquiry into the Principles of Distribution," Introduction.

by this critic of the individualistic system, but with some modification the challenge might be repeated to-day. And the answer would still have to be what a contemporary of Thompson, namely Hodgskin, thought it was. He declared that "the distress our people suffer — and the poverty we all complain of, is not caused by nature, but by some social institutions which either will not allow the laborer to exert his productive power, or which rob him of its fruits." [2]

Hodgskin demurred to the charge of the Ricardians that nature was at fault, that the law of diminishing returns explained everything, or that sexual passion gave civilization no chance. The socialists from Marx on have supported this criticism of the English radicals and pointed with an accusing finger to capitalism. The more modern view will not accept the whole of the socialistic indictment, but it is indisputably true that a change should and can be made.

The unequal distribution so far has been the result of innate differences between men, and of other differences less constant, more controllable. The superiorities of some will necessarily bring them victory in any battle. Physical strength and valor win in a hand-to-hand encounter. Great mental powers bring riches to men. But in addition we have had legal monopolies, the might of socio-economic organization gathered into a few hands, the ownership, by a small group, of natural resources which furnish the staples of consumption, and the right of inheritance, by which the wealthy could perpetuate their holdings not only in consumables but also in the rawstuffs. When the non-productive materials such as mineral and timber and soil fertility and water-power are deeded away to a few, whether by purchase or free gift

2 Hodgskin, Th., "Popular Political Economy," 1827; pp. 267–68.

does not matter, then unusual chances for gain are opened. Organization is the fruit of brain and property rights. It is virtually invincible, barring state action. We can defeat brain by itself, and there is always a method for controlling mere wealth. But let the two combine, and the partnership becomes nigh invincible.

The socialist has his eye on this combination, and desires to separate brain from monopoly in the extremely scarce resources of the world. He favors a redistribution of incomes to help the less gifted by nature, and in this he has the approval of science no less than of moral sentiments.

A theory of prosperity such as social science to-day recommends is incompatible with extremes in distribution. As long as income is a condition to leisure and education, as long as an economic leveling is a prerequisite to a feeling of fellowship in matters civic, moral, religious and intellectual, so long the juxtaposition of plutocrat and proletariat is full of menace. We *can* develop dormant powers of reasoning and of production or of enjoyment in man. This modern psychology and biology prove. We can produce more than we need to sustain the body. This history has shown. We can produce most by joint enterprise and capitalistic methods, meaning thereby roundabout methods and the use of machinery, no matter who owns it. Since then, according to the verdict of natural science health depends on food supplies and protection against bacterial diseases, and since an economic surplus is necessary to the specialization which makes modern science and discovery possible, it follows that wealth well distributed is most conducive to progress. The same economic interpretation of history which socialism first formulated as a sweeping law of evolution provides also part of our argument for urging equalization of fortunes.

Approximate leveling must be part of our plan for democratization of all rights and efforts.

However, we may look at the situation from another angle. We may emphasize the undoubted fact that distribution reacts upon production in two ways, viz., by affecting our choice of goods, and by influencing the volume of goods turned out, and that for these two reasons a marked concentration of income is reprehensible. This viewpoint has commonly been taken by socialists, and it agrees with the analysis of price advanced by professional economists. People disagree chiefly as to the place of competition in national productiveness.

That an extreme concentration of wealth must influence the enterpriser in his choice of goods to be produced should be self-evident. But if not, it follows logically from the very facts of utility and pricing which most economists content themselves to describe.

The rich will encourage the production of luxuries when millions lack the necessities. They will do this because of the principle of unlimited wants and of diminishing utility. They will do this because, in equalizing our margins of enjoyment of goods, we are able to offer different amounts of money for goods, once income is unevenly divided among the consumers. The prices are then for all the same, but the sacrifices are not. This is the circumstance that socialism most deplores.

Our wants are illimitable. Thanks to our imagination and power of inference we are able to wish for much more than we possess. We are never satisfied; which is on the whole a good thing. But since there seems always room for things besides those we already own and enjoy, we make *unequal* efforts or sacrifices to obtain additional goods when our possessions are unequal.

And we shall ask for *different* things, not merely for

larger amounts of any one article. We tire of one article as we increase our supply of it. We cease to value an over abundance of good things. Too much dinner sates our appetites. One or two musical instruments satisfy our longing for music. After we have bought so much of clothing or books or furniture we want no more of it, or we want very different types of each, so that we have virtually something different.

We therefore always spend our money deliberately in that we weigh the desirability of one commodity relative to another. We have options to buy things, but cannot ordinarily buy everything. We must decide what we want, how much of each class of goods, and in what order. If, for instance, a community has a supply of water it will allot it for different uses according to the total supply on hand. We may be sure that our thirst will first be quenched from the supply. We shall put drinking water before everything else. Then, if something is left, we shall perhaps use it for washing purposes and for the laundry. If still more remains we may decide to sprinkle the streets with it, so as to lay the dust. Or possibly our garden back of the house needs it, so we shall use it there. And only if all these needs are looked after shall we think of swimming pools, of public fountains and like details.

In some such order all our articles of consumption are used. An astonishing uniformity of tastes will manifest itself in the arrangement of broad classes of goods, however infinite the variations in detail. We all know what are the essentials of life on a physical plane. We all at first prefer clothing and shelter to bric-à-brac or sightseeing tours abroad. We cannot indulge in trivial comforts until a minimum for bodily sustenance is provided. Then, beyond that point, and in the finer grading of preferences, the individuality of the purchaser appears. The farmer does not value things like the urbanite. A clergyman has a scale of choices different from that of a hard manual worker or a scientist perchance. Our temperaments determine our choices. Some would have more food and others more books. Some will like to spend a great deal for pastimes, while others are eager to own a home first or to acquire a college education. Tastes differ in the particulars.

But let it be noted that the unequal division of wealth greatly accentuates the natural differences in taste. For now one man has much more to compare with his prospective purchase than the other. The rich man has a long line of wants already satisfied, consequently thinks little of his potential possessions, that is of his money. He will be willing to give much for trifles which the poor man dare not think of buying, since more important needs would then remain unfilled. The wealthy person thus is apt to demand goods which no one else wants, and which are not really a part of a sound standard of living. He will divert labor and material from employment that would raise the level of living of small earners to others which cannot raise it.

The overly rich are systematically catered to by all kinds of people anxious to earn a fat living irrespective of social welfare. As the saying is: Money talks and will command anything — and, one might add, will command to be obeyed. The rich man pays no more for the necessities than the poor because, being a rare exception, he cannot greatly influence popular demand, that is the majority of valuations and of costs in terms of sacrifice. He will pay ten cents for a pound of sugar, though he could give a hundred times that sum. Physicians, to be sure, have introduced a scale of fees proportionate to earnings real or alleged. This is at times held to be an act of justice. And it is, if we single out the services of the physician from all others as being more vital, and hence the most valuable to the poor who on a competitive basis might have to do without them. The scale of prices is therefore logical. But plainly, if all producers and sellers were to scale their prices according to the purchasing power of the customer, the end result would be simply the maintenance of present distribution. The adjusting of prices, including wages, to ability to pay would prevent a *further* concentration of wealth, particularly if it were made exactly and consistently for all services. But it could not abolish the present inequalities which socialism condemns.

The effect of a marked concentration of wealth on productiveness has been variously estimated. Some have held that it is an essential to maximum effort, while many others are convinced that the national income is thereby reduced.

Sidgwick, the noted English ethicist and economist, believed the former. He feared for the British level of living if the masses were to get their rights as the socialists saw them. He wrote: "Any great equalization of wealth would probably diminish the accumulation of capital on which the progress of industry depends; and would deteriorate the administration of the capital accumulated." [3] He was afraid, for one thing, of the people spending their additional earnings due to a redistribution of wealth. He no doubt thought that improvidence would get the better of common people and induce them to keep servants or make gluttons of themselves. The capital-fund, as defined by competitive economics, would thus shrink, and gradually the flow of concrete goods would end.

[3] Sidgwick, H., "Elements of Politics," p. 153.

Whether this is a good view to take of the habits of the average man is hard to say. We have no direct evidence to prove that socialism will decidedly increase the productive powers of the nation. But on the other hand we know of sumptuary laws and of education which have taught men moderation without hurting their feelings. In the end there will not be a great deal of waste because the ratio of capital to consumption goods is, with the exception of a good possibility for extending personal services almost indefinitely, fairly constant. It is really impossible to provide luxuries for those with large incomes unless they themselves or others save, that is see to the production of a suitable amount of capital which is to turn out the luxuries. Only a few may at any given time draw heavily upon their total nominal income in dollars and cents, the majority must be content with investments, so the future flow of consumables may grow.

As against this fact, however, we must acknowledge that personal services may easily expand unduly, for which reason partly an extreme concentration of wealth is undesirable. As has been shown elsewhere, socialism will increase our labor-power chiefly by making use of this principle. The hosts of men and women now employed in the rendering of trifling services will be turned into socially necessary workers, providing services more in keeping with the needs of the great majority, and rentiers will have to work also.

As socialists have often remarked, there are at present too many idlers feasting at a table set by others. Heirs and prospective heirs, the children of wealthy folk, grown up men and women, and not least of all married women in affluent circumstances, these are the parasites who depend upon others for their fat living. It is not the money earner himself who spends vast sums, but his family or relatives. Big producers at all times have been comparatively small consumers. Those who give most take the least, and gladly continue to give their services, or at any rate to follow their gainful pursuits. But consumption by proxy becomes a pleasant, because respectable, kind of a debauch. Habitual idleness thus perpetuates itself from one generation to the next.

Let us admit then that the socialist possibly has exaggerated the effects of the leisure class on national output. But if so he seems to have the better of it when defending his principle of collectivistic enterprise against the plea for competition which the friends of the present régime usually bring up first.

It has been argued that to decrease profits will mean a lowering of our level of living, because the average businessman will not do his best unless he can keep all he can get. The champions of ruthless individualism have again and again reverted to this position. It has seemed to them axiomatic that the present régime is efficient because the ablest are prodded on by rewards which socialism would withhold from them. If this be so, then of course competition should have no fetters, since the reduction of our income hampers progress, as socialists admit.

§ 3. **Private Property and Efficiency.**— But what is competition, and what has the past taught us in this respect? It is evident that much depends on the definition of our term, to say nothing of the bearing of experience on our topic.

Now, in the first place, one may retort with the irrefutable fact that the majority of the producers lack that supposedly necessary incentive already. The great majority of workers for a wage cannot increase income as they increase their output. Their day's work is roughly fixed, and their day's income is in most cases fixed exactly.

Piecework has been tried out, and many produce under that system to-day. But it has not always raised productivity, nor has the advantage of a larger output invariably offset the disadvantages in other lines. The indirect effects of speeding, whether urged by profit-sharing or by piece wages, have set both labor and legislators against it.

But, for that matter, it would be difficult to prove that men have produced poorly because they received a contractual income. Wages have not prevented us from raising our level of living more in the nineteenth century than before. Many hundreds of thousands have for years worked for salaries and done their best. Corporations have submitted to a restriction of earnings in percentages of their investment and not ceased therefore to serve the public. We have minimum prices and maximum wages, franchise taxes for net profits above a normal interest rate, and fees absolutely independent of demand or of values delivered. If a physician can pursue his practice without charging all the traffic will bear, why should not a business firm selling rawstuffs or finished goods? It would seem that either we have to divide the population into two groups, namely the greedy and the generous, or else redefine our concept of competition. If, and to the extent that, it is true that some will exert themselves only for the pelf to be gained, while others find their reward in something besides pelf, incomes should be uncontrolled in one case, and curbed in another. But this is not the most obvious way of meeting our dilemma.

Rather it should be plain that competition involves much more than a lust for maximum earnings. Hodgskin, whom we have quoted several times before, wrote: "I can understand how a right to appropriate the produce of other men, under the name of interest or profit, may be a stimulus to cupidity, but I cannot understand how lessening the reward of the laborer, to add to the wealth of the idle, can increase industry or accelerate the progress of society in wealth."[4] This is one kind of rebuttal the socialist might use. But the more scientific one is a correct analysis of the competitive spirit.

Competition is not simply a struggle for riches, as economics frequently has made it out to be; nor is it a trial of the pyx by which the pure is separated from the impure.

The fittest in society is not the fittest among animals. This is the first now universally recognized fact which the individualist has to remember. Evolution is not progress, for man has developed powers of speech and of reasoning, of memory and of associations, which permitted him to master nature rather than live by exploiting his fellowmen. When man began to unfold his learning faculties and to wrest from nature her innermost secrets he was in a fair way to substitute surplus for deficit, and to displace internecine strife by intellectual research.

Or we may put the matter thus.

Competition originally had to do with sex and self preservation in a struggle for sheer existence, but later on other factors became more important. Altruism had always been a natural concomitant of sexual reproduction and of parental responsibilities. From it the first unselfish instincts must have gathered strength. But gradually the enlargement of the individual's environs developed group consciousness in addition to blood ties. The selfish instincts of pugnacity and acquisitiveness which relate closely to the reproductive functions were tempered by feelings for others. A solidarity of interests arose and was cultivated by the requisites of production. Division of labor and technical coöperation could mean nothing

[4] Hodgskin, *op. cit.*, p. 254.

else, however stimulating in some respects it was for the most individualistically inclined. As the material level rose the so-called moral did, too. Passion came to be blended with compassion, self-assertion with a susceptibility to the approval of outsiders, and the vying for booty with the penchant for achievement. The whole course of civilization is a conversion of the physical self into a social self, and of products into personality.

The cave-man is still with us, but not in large numbers. He is likely to be a movie hero, or a felon in prison. The pirate of old has turned profiteer perhaps, but most of the profiteers are producers nonetheless. The marauders of the economic world no longer pillage and destroy merely; they also build or replace in part what they have undone. The chieftain who led his hordes into the bloody fray has given way to the business magnate who excels in the managing of labor forces. Not all highwaymen have died out to leave us unmolested, but the surviving must be clever to elude the law, or they must give a quid pro quo of some kind.

In other words competition, if it ever was merely a struggle for loot, has long ceased to be such. In modern times it has increasingly meant a desire to create as well as a bent for acquisition. The hardest fighters do not want the enjoyment of their possessions. They do not feast at banquets or spend their day in carousals. The most competitively spirited compete for power which wealth brings, for the prestige that it means, but also for the joy of the game.

We love to compare our deeds. Competition is this vying for superiority regardless of emoluments. It is not merely the seeking after rare things money can buy. Some scarcities not in the money market are equally entrancing, and most of them stand for social order.

People do their utmost because energy needs a vent. Or they plod along from habit, doing day by day their duty, perhaps unthinkingly. Habit and energy, pride in achievements and the instinct for approval, these are the elements in competition that count more in the aggregate than the lust for profits.

Men wish to identify themselves with a piece of work. They crave leadership or distinction measurable by individual creations. Socialism, therefore, should put a premium of praise and a badge of distinction on the exceptional deed. This all statesmanship will respect, and within a limited sphere always has applied. If under socialism the exceptional producers are permitted to do their own work, to follow up their conceptions and endeavors, to bring to public notice what they have done, then the curtailment of profits will do no great harm. It will not restrain the most meritorious, though some may desist at the outset. Socialists should make sure of connecting men with their work wherever possible and in such a way that the two may be identified. It is this which the finest of men will wish. Incentive to produce by mastering the subject, and by demonstrating the results to an admiring or at least to a sympathetic public — such is the most fundamental significance of competition. Men of preëminence always will lead. The right to lead and to do substantially as we please in creating values will remain for all times to come. We cannot abolish it by a fiat of law. But the right to earn as much as, and by any method, we please is bound to be circumscribed the more, the more advanced scientific thought.

It might be objected that taxation can take the place of socialization, so our present régime may be left intact. This thought has often been broached, and of course contains much truth. But it should also be remembered that the final result of greatly increased taxation cannot but be a curb to individual enterprise.

Taxes are never the most desirable means for rectifying distributive errors, for to take taxes is to admit that somebody *owns*, and this implied or explicit admission of earnings on the part of the tax payer is an injustice to the bulk of the wage earners. In the second place, taxation is a roundabout way of leveling incomes, much as Prohibition once labored indirectly because it agitated against *consumption* long before it argued against the production of liquors. Indirect methods of that sort mean leakage and lost motion. They mean uncertainties and protests that are falsely grounded.

But, in the third place, it is difficult to see what the central or local governments would do with the receipts if they were to take from the rich by taxes what socialism wishes to give the masses of the people more directly. A revenue four or five times as large as now needed for routine administration would call for investments in an unusual way. In the United States, for instance, the total public revenue, federal and local, was for the year 1912 equal to about six per cent. of the social dividend. For every dollar of national income the authorities collected six cents in taxes. If the socialistic principles of leveling were to be realized by taxation the revenue would approximate twenty per cent. or more of the total national income. This would possibly look like a nice gain for both government and the poor man who was taxed little or nothing. But what would be done with the receipts? They would either have to be redistributed directly among the most needy, or they would mean a vast extension of government functions with the result that enterprise would increasingly become a public business. Taxation consonant with the distributive norms of socialism would thus lead to government ownership anyway.

§ 4. **Pricing under Socialism.**— Socialism, however, would mean more than the socialization of capital. It would not merely prevent the rich from becoming richer, but in addition it plans a revaluation of goods and services, so that none *can* earn the huge sums which now are said to represent their "product." Under socialism there will be no inheritance of capital, and only limited inheritance of consumers' goods. This source of rentals then being taken away, and the work of all being valued at a new scale, incomes would not vary a great deal, though some differences would continue to exist. But at any rate the incomes would all be earned. Rent, interest, and profits would have no place in the new régime. All producers would be wage-earners. All workers, no matter what their profession or trade, would receive wages by stipulation with the government. The aleatory gains of the entrepreneur would end, and contractual earnings would alone prevail.

It would of course be possible to ration out the goods which each worker or head of a family is entitled to. Instead of paying him in token money with which to purchase his needs he could be paid in amounts of commodities constituting the value of his labors. In this way the government, or the locally managed public industries, would know exactly what to produce of each kind of good, and the possibilities of foolish spending were removed. To apportion income in this manner has some advantages particularly when we are dealing with irresponsible parties. But it also offers great administrative difficulties, and besides, it has not been seriously proposed by socialists. It is intended, if one may judge by the dominant tone of writings on this neglected subject, to retain the use of money in so far as it serves simply as a medium of exchange. Money will be chiefly a claim to values without having itself intrinsic value. Paper money will predominate. It will, like poker chips in a game of cards, represent titles to real values, but will have none itself. And trade thus will mean only a moving of goods. Commerce will at bottom mean regional distribution involving the transportation of commodities. The public central warehouses will supply the stores at which the consumer cashes in his token money. The exchange of goods for services rendered will thus be simplified, and much duplication of effort stop.

But at what *rates* will goods exchange? Price is a ratio of exchange. If a bushel of wheat sells to-day for two dollars which buy five pounds of meat, the price of a bushel of wheat is five pounds of meat. Value is price when values are exchanged. Price is the amount of one article given for a unit amount of another, that unit being most commonly known as money. The dollar, e. g., is the unit in terms of which the American people measure their exchange ratios.

Their are four possibilities of pricing, one of which socialism will adopt. We may fix the price of commodities, but not the wages paid for services. We may fix the wage, but not the price of commodities. We may fix both prices for commodities and wages. And finally we may fix neither prices nor incomes, that is wages.

At last analysis of course all prices are incomes, and vice versa. If I buy a pair of shoes I have to pay a price, and if a clerk sells them to me he also charges his employer a price for his work. The employer calls the wage of the clerk a price which forms part of his business expenses; but the clerk speaks of wages as income.

To him it is coming in, though for the owner of the store it is going out. Income and outgo constitute couples that in practice cannot be separated into individual acts. But according to viewpoint one and the same value is either price or income. A price contains the incomes of all those involved in the creation of the article back of the price. In a pair of shoes, for instance, are incorporated many incomes, which in minute amounts went to all those who helped make the shoe, from farm hand tending the steer that furnished the hide to the clerk in the store selling the finished article.

At present the great bulk of prices, i. e., of prices for commodities and of incomes for services, are determined competitively. We have an open market, and let the forces of supply and demand decide what a commodity shall sell for. This is the theory on which the science of economics proceeded to correlate product and income, and in large measure this is actual fact. However, purely competitive pricing has ceased in many fields of production and exchange. Monopoly has supplanted competition, and public regulation has put limits to both competitive and monopoly-pricing. We might therefore acknowledge frankly that to-day public control of prices is gaining, though competition still holds part of the field. Freight rates and the price of coal or bread are publicly fixed. Urban traction companies may not earn more than a certain per cent. on their investment, and employees of the government of course have as such a publicly set annual income. If necessary their salaries will be adjusted to labor conditions in private business, but roughly speaking the government fixes a wage without regard to competition from outside. Against this rule, however, must be placed the unionization of labor, the upshot of which is the determination of all wages by agreement with the employer. Hence a growing part of wage-earners reduces the force of individual competition and puts in place of it what socialism virtually aims at, namely payment in accord with public opinion. A socialistic wage-law will, like any act of legislature, meet the sanction of the majority, but public opinion will be guided from the headquarters of business.

Incomes under socialism will be fixed per work hour or per year, but the prices of commodities will vary with demand just as they do to-day. This seems to be the plan advocated by most defenders of the new order. Consumers will be allowed to bid for goods as they do now, but in the first place there will be minima and maxima, and in the second place the effect upon production will not be the present one, because incomes will be put more nearly on a par with each other.

From the standpoint of adjustment of supply to demand, however, the free pricing of goods will under socialism have nothing ahead of the now prevailing system. Nor does there seem any way out of the difficulty unless a rationing of goods takes the place of purchase with money paid by the government for services. If, namely, the government sets prices too high the people may not buy, or buy but little, so that great stocks are left at the end of the year which cannot be used up. But if prices are set too low, the demand will exceed supplies on hand, and, unless maxima prices are decreed, a ruthless bidding will set in. Even though incomes are equally or fairly evenly assigned, many then will still go without the goods they should have as part of a right standard of living. Tastes differ enormously. The ideal of public welfare can only be guarded by specifying all those articles which are part of a normal level of living, and the use of which in stated maximum and minimum amounts is publicly recommended or ordered. But in either case supply and demand will not agree closely. And if no price fixation is planned the discrepancy will be even greater. There will always be too much of some commodities and not enough of others. It will not be possible to ascertain beforehand what people want. The averages of demand will be discovered slowly, and perhaps change as fast as they have been tabulated for use in production. At present a delicate mechanism of exchange, wholesale and retail, attends to the equilibration which is never perfect, but moves not too far from the median line of adjustment. We have trade journals and government crop reports, international news service and statistical surveys privately conducted. We have brokers and bourses looking after the fluctuations of supply and demand. There is buying and selling in the harvest field, and of harvested crops for delivery many months ahead. And most important of all, we have the pressure of rising prices and the license of falling prices, by which device demand is suited to supplies and price is suited to willingness to pay, the poorest dropping out of the market first.

It is not likely that socialistic organization will do much better in this respect, than the one now in effect. It will be far more just to the average consumer, but it will not avoid altogether the waste attending the distribution of goods over large areas, among many millions of people. Nor will it be easy to obtain rawstuffs at short notice from abroad, in case demand moves that way, or to find labor in the home market to increase the supply of particular articles. The more socialism seeks to internationalize levels of living, the more it will have to reckon with waste, and with sacrifices for those nations which are most prosperous and technically best administered.

§ 5. **Costs under Socialism.**— In so far, however, as

demand is not to fix the price of commodities another principle will doubtless be invoked, and socialists have often spoken of costs in this connection. It has by some been hinted that goods will be sold at cost, and by others that costs will measure roughly the price of goods. But how far may this rule really be enforced?

As to sales at cost, the phrase is misleading if it is to convey the thought of prices below the present, because no profits will be made. The sale at cost would be no gain, because socialistic costs would comprise more or less than competitive costs, according as we look at them.

In general cost is a ratio. Budgets are ratios of income and outgo, and cost and return are the two aspects of this mutual relation. If, for instance, I lose one bushel of seedwheat in producing five bushels of harvested wheat I may say that the cost of the five bushels is the one bushel put into the ground. Cost is outgo measured in terms of income, and the rate of return (or the profit) is income compared with outgo.

Cost may be expressed either in goods, by weight and volume, or in money. The example of wheat just given is one of cost measurement by weight and tale. But instead of referring the five bushels of wheat harvested to one bushel of seed I might also have reckoned the return by the *time* it took to produce them. I might have said: I produced five bushels in four months. Next year I shall try to produce them in three months, and I shall then have increased my rate of return or decreased my costs. The time element evidently is sometimes important for cost accounting, and it figures prominently in national budgets. But we might, in the third place, measure rates of return or costs by income per capita of the population. If the output of wheat per capita is ten bushels in one year, and twelve the next, we may call this gain the equivalent of cost reduction. We may feel that it reduces our cost of living. We may measure our purchasing power in that way, and feel downcast or elated according to productiveness per average inhabitant.

But if we pass over to the competitive norm, the rate of return in concrete goods becomes less significant than the income of dollars and cents per outgo of the same. The farmer, thus, may not care whether he grows more wheat per acre, or even more wheat per outlay in goods and services. He may simply ask: What will I get in money for money spent? If I grow less wheat, but sell it at a higher price I shall have raised my profits. My costs will be relatively lower. My income having grown while my expenses remained constant, my expenses have practically shrunk.

The correct analysis of cost thus leads us to the conclusion which Marx himself could not escape, but on the contrary placed candidly before his readers. To wit, socialism cannot decrease costs unless it raises efficiency. It will not really confer a benefit upon the consumer, though nominally it sells commodities at cost. The list of costs will have changed. The names may not be the old. But the ratio of income to outgo for the nation as a whole is no better except invention and organization reduce the outgo of effort and material relative to returns in material.

There will be probably no insurance of capital such as we know to-day. There will be no profits going to a small group of entrepreneurs. But there will be the outgo of raw-materials, of wages in the shape of goods, most of it being paid to the producers of concrete commodities or of personal services, but some of it to officials looking after the non-economic duties such as maintenance of army, of the department of justice, etc. There will furthermore be reserves for unforeseen losses, for replacement of capital goods, for expansion of business when and where necessary, and for charity and pensions. The cripples in body or mind will be taken care of, and the aged will receive regular remittances which will be paid out of prices and products figuring in socialistic costs.

But the costs, though determinable in general, will not be measurable for a particular article. The use of machinery precludes such a possibility, and besides, there is the joint product, the by-product, for which costs cannot be computed except very indirectly. The imputation of values to services and to commodities will be as arbitrary under socialism as it ever was. The number of hours it took to create a certain article or its value will in most cases not be ascertainable, since many men have worked together and simultaneously to produce it, to say nothing of overhead expenses and the costs in work hours, of machinery and management and of particular inventions basic to the productive act.

Prices, in fine, will be fixed somewhat arbitrarily to agree with the ideals of living. The socialistic standard of living will keep some articles cheap so all may buy them, and raise the price of high grade luxuries, supposing they are produced at all.

§ 6. **The Socialistic Principle of Distribution.**— To assure the average man a decent livelihood prices for services too will be put nearly on one plane. The revaluation will not only cheapen necessities, but it will give the humblest laborer a return in wages sufficient for all approved wants. *Socialism will measure productivity by work hours.* The worker, with certain exceptions, will be paid according to the time he puts in at the work bench. It will be assumed that the rate of work, that is of actual achievement, is for men in like occupations uniform, even though some differences may in practice appear. No other method for valuating services can exist under socialism. Ten hours of work will be worth twice as much as five hours.

Exceptions will do justice to striking differences in the nature of work done. Inventors and novelists, for instance, will be rewarded in a lump sum, or on the installment plan, for creations of unusual and abiding merit. Managers will receive more than underlings. Those highly trained in science or skilled in handicrafts will have more to spend than crude labor. But the latter will at least have enough for a living standardized by the objective tests of individual and social welfare. It will, in general, be argued as Adam Smith did a hundred and fifty years ago, that "by nature a philosopher is not in genius and disposition half so different from a street porter, as a mastiff is from a greyhound —."[5] This viewpoint will guide the socialist. He will emphasize resemblance in men more than their differences. He will seek to democratize effort and rights. He will differentiate with care, but tolerate no extremes of income. Unlike services, but approximately like pay for all! The brainiest will give, and the numskulls will take. Those who now by mere cunning and astuteness garner riches will obtain less. What they lack in creativeness will reduce their income as much as now the possession of shrewdness raises it above the average.

Distribution according to need will, if necessary, take the place of distribution according to number of hours at work. The least gifted will get more than their product even as measured by socialism. The standard of living will be raised for the masses. It will include many items

[5] "Wealth of Nations," Book I, Chapter 2. See also Thompson, W., "Inquiry into the Principles of Distribution," p. 4.

not now figuring in a wage-earner's budget, and it will allot some of the essentials in a somewhat better proportion than seems now practicable.

A Minimum Wage Board recently estimated the wage necessary for self-supporting women in the printing industry at sixteen dollars a week. This in the summer of 1919! It wished to be just, and itemized the expenses for each class of wants. It did the best it could to allow for all essentials, and the showing is not bad at first glance. But when one notices that for charity and organization (union-fee?) each it allowed per year five dollars, for the services of physician or dentist or oculist twenty-five, and about thirty dollars for recreation, amusement, and self-improvement, one wonders how much solace the adjustment really brought to the workers. Sixteen dollars a week is not enough by any norm of living scientifically sanctioned. It may be the best possible under prevailing conditions, but it cannot satisfy our sense of fairness, or the demands of those who compare individual earnings with the aggregate social dividend.

Actual needs are not, furthermore, the same for all people. If distribution is to meet needs rather than productivity — however measured — the differences in men and their occupations will have to be duly considered. It will be one of the trying questions of socialism to find out what is best for different people. When the variety of goods is as great as in modern times the individuality of taste has plenty of room for exhibition. There will be differences according to temperament or sex, according to age and condition of body and mind, according to climate and season, and according to types of occupation. It is not simply a matter of preferences such as may properly be ignored, but rather of habits the indulgence in which may play a vital part in the productiveness of the worker. It is a matter first of educating tastes correctly by positive and negative means of control, and secondly of adjusting the price of goods so that variety of taste may be met to the satisfaction of the largest number. For this reason price fixation will have but limited usefulness. It will be the duty of socialists to permit the individual as much freedom in his purchase as seems to agree with his personal welfare or with social efficiency, but just where the two conflict it will not always be easy to determine.

CHAPTER VIII

THE LIMITS IN CONSUMPTION

§ 1. **The Nature of Consumption.**— The subject of consumption occupies a peculiar place in the history of economic thought. It has from early times on been regarded as an integral part of the science of economics, and yet its treatment has varied greatly. Some have viewed consumption as a value aspect, some have appended it to treatises with the thought of showing the bearing of extravagance on public revenues. Some have given it scant courtesy in a discussion of wages, and others have made it the key to distributive facts in general.

It does not matter what consumption means to the orthodox economist. The socialist is professedly governed by the ethical interpretation which Ruskin summed up sententiously if obscurely, in the phrase: "There is no wealth but life." What life, we ask?

Socialism has helped men to find the objective tests of social prosperity. It also has promoted a fitting regard for the non-economic expressions of economic principles. But some limits of consumption remain that socialists often overlook, or deem extraneous to their subject matter.

Consumption should not be defined primarily as a loss of values incurred in the production of other values, or as destruction of values or of physical things, though the destruction of food for instance has deep significance for the farmer who must replace it annually. A great many commodities are not used up in the act of consumption, books and paintings and musical compositions and radium and water power being examples. On the other hand, wealth will deteriorate and crumble whether we use it or not, and values competitively calculated may shrink and expand, for instance the price of stocks, independent of even the influence of weathering.

The real meaning of consumption from a social standpoint is *use for reaction physical and psychic.* Whatever we react upon is part of our environment. Whatever we respond to has been in a sense an item for our consumption. To consume by responding to stimuli, this is the gravamen of life. Social science can do no more than study the relation of stimuli from without and from within in so far as they proceed from, or influence, our wealth relations. Consumption is the act of absorbing and assimilating things economic, food being converted into blood, communication into knowledge applied, experiments into habits becoming second nature. *Consumption is the process socially directed by which product is converted into personality.*

§ 2. **Consumption and Human Nature.**— But the efforts of consumption on human nature are not measurable in the degree that socialists have now and then believed. The economic interpretation of history may emphasize the relation between economic income and psychic outgo, but it should not induce us to expect the impossible. Evolution is a process almost too slow for human comprehension. We might indicate its course by a line a foot long and then add a wee speck to mark the historical epoch of which man is, through records more or less reliable, a witness. The momentum of that long line of tendencies is so great that no one century of reform can overcome it. We must not count on the mutability of human nature, because eons of time have gradually made it what it is. The economic interpretation of the past is right when, judging by present experiences, it traces an interrelation between environment and man, between food conditions and physique or mental development; but it errs if it ascribes to our historical economics an influence over the shaping of human traits. These traits are much older than history. They cannot be re-made by environmental control, but only be used in such ways as will suit the needs of the moment.

Socialism will not change human nature, though it turn upside down the present order of things. The Lamarckian thought of the transmission of acquired characters has not so far met with a cordial reception, though it has been put to many tests and made some friends among authorities. For one thing, socialism is little affected by the acceptance or rejection of Lamarckianism; for another the doctrine is, in its original and most consequential form, discarded by modern biology.

Socialists like social scientists in general can afford to ignore the Lamarckian idea because it revolves about periods of time in which contemporary science is not directly interested. If acquired traits were immediately hereditary in a determinable way the socialist would have to *create his economic environment for each generation anew,* so as to offset what traits might have been transmitted from parent to offspring. Either he does this, or he must stabilize his environment so completely that all inherited traits originated in an environment would suit all future environments. But since life is continuous change through interaction, and since all man-made environment changes from decade to decade, the adjustment for each generation would have to be made independent of the prior one. New characters, new economic conditions, this would be the recipe.

But it appears at once that such a rapid acquisition of traits would, first, make man much less stable than we know him to be, and secondly, would give the reformer no advantage, since good traits might speedily degenerate into undesirable ones through a lack of proper environment control during one single generation. The breeder of animals and plants would be similarly embarrassed if Lamarckianism were so construed, and eugenics, of course, could never hope to evolve a right mankind, because many uncontrollable environmental influences would botch his selections and cultures.

So it can only be a question as to what the environment accomplishes in the long run, say in the course of millions of years. This view of Lamarckianism seems the only logical one and has been given wide recognition by experts.

§ 3. **The Biological View of Environment.**— A biologist of note has defined an acquired character as a "structural change in the body of a multicellular organism, involving a deviation from the normal and induced during the individual lifetime by a change in environment or in function, and such that it transcends the limits of organic elasticity and therefore persists after the factors inducing it have ceased to operate." [1] In other words, the proof of transmission by organic descent of an acquired trait is the fact that it continues to function after the factors responsible for its emergence have disappeared. If the son acts as the father did, because of traits aroused by the father's environment which, however, does *not* act on the son, then the particular trait is inherited and the acquired one has become organic. The precise problem of biology is: Does such a transmission commonly take place? Is the effect of environment upon offspring

[1] Thompson, J. A., "Heredity," p. 173.

specific or general, direct through the germ-cell or indirect via the body-cell, cumulative or non-cumulative in the sense that the inherited trait is not intensified without further environmental influences?

Now, the facts of cytology advise us against the acceptance of Lamarckianism. The view "that the germ-plasm responds directly to the experiences of the body has no substantial evidence in its support." And the writer of these words adds: "I know of course that the whole Lamarckian school rests its argument on the assumption that the germ-plasm responds to all profound changes in the soma; but despite the very large literature that has grown up dealing with this matter proof is still lacking. And there is abundant evidence to the contrary."[2]

Experiments speak in favor of, rather than against, Weismann's doctrine of non-inheritance. The impossibility of knowing, especially as regards human beings, whether a trait is really congenital, and whether certain environmental data are essential in the development of an inherited trait acquired by the parent, militates indirectly against Lamarckianism. But the facts first gathered by Mendel, the Austrian amateur biologist, in his experiments with the edible pea have enlarged our understanding of the functions of bi-sexual reproduction so that to-day, after years of investigation, agreement seems to have been reached on the points most significant for social science.

The seat of heredity has been traced to minute, ultra-microscopic entities imbedded in the chromosomes which in turn are part of the nucleus of every germ cell. It is held that such unit factors must exist because without them the results of hybridization remain inexplicable,

[2] Morgan, Th. H., "Heredity and Sex," p. 17.

while with them nearly the whole mystery of heredity, sex determination not excepted, appears solved. Three postulates, according to an eminent authority, lie back of the doctrine of unit-factors which determine plant and animal traits, including those of the specie homo sapiens. Namely the assumption that the factors are constants, that two factors for each trait are lodged in the cell, and that these factors segregate, or remain segregated in the maturing germ-cell. Grant this, as the facts of the case urge us to, and the riddle of inheritance offers no insurmountable difficulties. As Professor Morgan puts it: "The validity of the unit-factor conception rests upon the fact that whenever (as often happens) all other conditions, external and internal that modify characters, remain constant, then clear-cut ratios are obtained which can be explained only as due to segregation, in definite ways, of particular hereditary factors that perpetuate themselves unchanged from generation to generation." [3]

The "factor" in the chromosome therefore is the fashioner of human traits and in a sense, of history. Human traits are built out of them, and each factor affects others while it in turn may be affected from several sides. "A single factor may have several effects, and a single character may depend on many factors—." [4] But "the real unit in heredity is the factor, while the character is the product of a number of genetic factors and of environmental conditions." [5] Which is to say, what practically all geneticists admit, that the influence of the environment is real, though indeterminate and indirect. To quote once more from Professor Morgan: "There is a small amount of evidence, very incomplete and insufficient

[3] Morgan, Th. H., "The Mechanism of Mendelian Heredity," p. 47.
[4] *Ibidem*, p. 210.
[5] *Ibidem*.

at present, to show that changes in the environment reach through the soma and modify the germinal material." [6] The extreme view, therefore, that "by the shuffle and deal of the hereditary factors in the formation of two of these cells in fertilization our hereditary natures were forever sealed —" [7] should give way to more moderate notions of a primary influence working hand in hand with a secondary from outside.

The fundamental fact is the interaction of the determiners in the chromosomes. Each factor will bear on the other. "An overstatement to the effect that each factor may affect the entire body is less likely to do harm than to state that each factor affects only a particular character." [8] But in addition we have the circuitous route of outside forces in reaching the germ-cell. Human nature *is* affected from the outside, by post-natal experiences, so that the offspring will manifest the result; but the effects are general. No ratio between experience and variation in particular traits can be established. "The effect is general rather than specific, and the result as seen in the offspring has no discoverable correlation with any particular part or structure of the parental soma." [9]

Furthermore, the number of possible combinations by these factors is so immense that, if their shuffling and permutations fashion the characters recognized by man, it is well possible to obtain countless shades and variations, even supposing the environment had no force whatsoever. The chief result of bisexual reproduction is a

[6] Morgan, Th. H., "Heredity and Sex," p. 18.

[7] Conklin, E. G., "Heredity and Environment," p. 463. (I. Edit.)

[8] Morgan. Th. H., "Critique of the Theory of Evolution," p. 72.

[9] Guyer, M. F., "Being Wellborn," p. 135. Similarly Thorndike, E. L., "Educational Psychology," Volume III, p. 310. But for a leading authority against the Weismannian view see Cope, E. D., "Primary Factors of Organic Evolution," especially pp. 392-443.

much greater diversification of traits than a sexual life permitted. But it also brings about the ratios first observed by Mendel, and other ratios which, though originally interpreted as exceptions to the rule, soon were explained as results of combinations unsuspected by Mendel. In the long run, on the principle of chance variations, regularity in appearance of traits was inevitable. Dependent upon the number of factors, and upon their bundling in the formation of unit-characters, parents would bequeath traits to their offspring in fixed proportion. Per thousand or million of inhabitants such and such traits would recur with astonishing regularity. Indeed, the logical bearing of the laws of probability and error upon genetics has been acknowledged with enthusiasm in support of eugenic programs. In the words of one geneticist: "Nothing is clearer than that the inevitable consequences of bisexual reproduction and of the manner of growth by the halving of the cell-contents is to insure that character-combinations, effected in this manner, are brought together in definite mathematical proportions not far from those expressed in the expansion of the binomial. This is the real foundation of Mendel's law for characters that do not blend, and it also expresses the relative proportions of characters that do blend." [10]

The latter is the most important point for socialism. It does not matter whether a human trait is deemed a unit in the cytological sense or not. All traits recur on the principle of average and frequency of errors as mathematicians understand the terms. "The differences in hereditary endowment — of strength or intelligence, of stature or longevity, of fertility or social disposition, have a certain regularity of distribution, so far as we can

[10] Davenport, E., "Principles of Breeding," p. 546.

measure them at all. They conform to what is called the Normal Law of Frequency —."[11] In this sense, therefore, *human nature is constant.* Our experiences in everyday life are confirmed. Historians hear their own verdict repeated, and reformers know what not to expect from reforms.

It is not likely that the abolition of private property will affect posterity through the living generation, except by way of social heredity. Organic heredity will play no part in the change. Genius will be more plentiful perhaps, and certainly types of subnormality ought to become rarer, but we can no more measure a crop of genius by economic income than we can improve the human race unerringly by the application of genetics to society.

In the case of genius we have still to acknowledge that the occupation of parents and grandparents seems to have exercised no measurable influence upon the direction genius took, and that the characteristics of one economic period have never given us a clue as to the sorts of genius born in the next epoch. We only know that superior civilizations have excelled in the production of genius, and that these titans of intellect themselves advanced the thought of their age. We do not know whether genius is a mutation in the biological sense, or whether it should be classed as a normal fluctuation, non-hereditary and insignificant for evolutionary purposes.

Fluctuations have been defined as continuous variations "which are graded, the extremes being connected by a complete series of intermediate conditions."[12] A Mutation according to one authority, is "a discontinuous

[11] Thompson, J. A., "Heredity" (2nd Edit.), p. 523.
[12] Castle, W. E., "Genetics and Eugenics," p. 56.

germinal change arising from a physical or chemical alteration in the structure of the organism, or of one or both of the germ-cells which produce a new individual, or from such a change arising in certain cells elsewhere in the life-cycle of the organism, this change being capable of complete inheritance at least in some of the offspring, although reversion may occur in others."[13] What is known of genius might be classed with either definition, but it does not matter much because mental traits are not known to be subject to Mendelian laws of heredity. The cultivation of genius, that is of types of men most influential in the development of races, cannot as yet be considered a subject for science.

The scope and usefulness of eugenics is, in fact, seriously limited by several gaps in our knowledge of the organism. We do not know exactly what constitutes a human unit character, though it is agreed that a single mental trait is compounded of probably many factors in the germ-cell.[14] It is of first importance to ascertain the correlation of good characters, or of the good with the bad, so the latter may be culled out if possible; but the data for such procedure are altogether lacking. It is admitted that human beings, unlike lower forms of life, continue to grow mentally long after physical growth has stopped. In many cases mentality develops most rapidly after the mating age has normally passed, say from the thirtieth year on. It would therefore be a mistake to judge the fitness or excellence of a mating couple purely by its qualifications at the date of marriage. And again, the means of detecting inherent faults and of regulating marriage are exceedingly uncertain. It will always be

13 Gates, R. R., "The Mutation Factor in Evolution."

14 See e.g., Thorndike, E. L., "Educational Psychology," Volume III, p. 268.

difficult to accomplish in the breeding of humans what the animal breeder has already achieved.

And finally there will be much disputing as to what the desired type of manhood or womanhood is. What kind of man is wanted? This is the paramount question which the combined training of natural and social scientists may not enable us to answer. There exist no records by which we may be guided. Each group of experts will describe the ideal man, and in many points the agreement of groups will be ample.[15] But on others no unanimity will be reached. History and sociology only teach the predominance of several types of men, and the apparent necessity of a large number of types for the attainment of unusual things. Civilization needs many kinds of people. Specialization should not be counselled merely as a precept in education, but if it were possible the eugenist should seek to produce strains highly specialized, so our learning period may be shortened or natural aptitude bring greater results.

A change of the proportion in which different types of men now are born must plainly have a momentous effect upon future history. But the eugenist seems as helpless in this matter as the socialist. Both must acknowledge their limitations. Genetics has not yet furnished us a clue to the elimination of all the unfit, and socialism cannot hope to root out all evils in social life by rooting out private capital. Socialists, however, have the advantage in that the direct and indirect influence of the environment upon the living organism is known and often measurable. Socialists will always have a large field for

[15] For leading classifications of People according to dominant traits see, for instance, Ratzenhofer, G., "Soziologische Erkenntnis"; Patten, S. N., "Development of English Thought"; and Giddings, F. H., "Inductive Sociology."

action regardless of what eugenics may claim for itself. The more fickle human nature, the more important a right economic environment for each living generation. The more constant human nature, the more pressing manifestly our duty to adapt man to his environment and to redirect his inclinations as the facts of social science advise. The economist, like the socialist, cannot lose by any answer finally given to the Lamarckian query, but in the light of current investigations the necessity of sound economy and of wise government seems more obvious than ever before. The variables lie outside of man viewed socially, for while variation is fully as significant as heredity, the law of probability applied to the workings of the hereditary mechanism assures us of a fairly constant distribution of departures from type. Some traits are shared by all men. The instincts may be classed among them, though their degree of strength varies. About the more universal we group the less universal human traits. Special deviations occur, but not frequently. The more marked a deviation the rarer it is. Thus the core of human nature seems to remain the same. Doubtless it only seems to, for everything changes, the fundamental traits of man not excluded. But the change is so gradual that we do not notice it. It is as with the sun which is said to move toward a far out point in the cosmos. We picture it in motion, and yet make it a constant because of the revolution and rotation of the earth, which is so much more in evidence. We ignore the movement of the central body and heed only those of our own planet. Human nature may be called a constant for much the same reason.

§ 4. **Income and Efficiency.**— What we can do with men by raising their income is a problem each generation must solve anew,[16] but the uncontrollable recurrence of types manifestly sets bounds to our reforms. We should not expect to double efficiency because we double library facilities, and we should not guarantee people happiness because we have added to their creature comforts. The powers of response to economic stimuli such as goods embody cannot be arbitrarily developed, though something may be done with them. The circumstance that all experiences are interrelations should convince us of the fatuity of adjustments in one quarter only. It takes more than one element in education to arouse our dormant faculties, and it takes many combinations of personal traits and objective facts to make man contented. Perhaps we shall succeed in mastering some of them, but not all.

In so far as the end of consumption is the development of innate powers for action, a sufficient economic income is of course a prerequisite. But since only that is part of our world which we react to, consciously or unconsciously, much income is sure to be wasted. It will bring no psychic returns. It may under special direction be used to stimulate reactions and intensify them, but in itself it may remain inert. Either the initiative is inborn, or it must come from outside through the facts of sociation in general and of education in particular.

Nothing is more familiar than the sight of people who command wealth, but stand helpless not knowing what to do with it. People are surrounded with art treasures, but derive no benefit from them. Opportunity beckons them on all sides, but they will not be inspired. Exten-

[16] The effect of social environment on genius and achievement is stressed notably by Ward, L. F., in his "Pure Sociology," and in his later "Applied Sociology," where Chapter 9 deals with an eminent French study on this subject.

sive travels yield no lasting productive impressions. They see but do not understand. They listen, but do not heed. They *associate* with the best, but fail to *assimilate* the best. Suggestions come to them from all sides, but nothing valuable is constructed out of them.

Many scientists worked without funds or apparatus and laboratory, yet they opened up new and large fields of investigation the results of which we call modern civilization. It is not the number of facts mastered by Aristotle that put him in a class by himself, for many a youth today has more of them at his fingers' ends than the inventor of the syllogism had ever heard of. Rather it was what he put into the few facts he knew, the meaning he gave them by properly correlating them, and the rules of conduct he deduced from them in his search for a richer life. A Newton could invent calculus to solve self-imposed problems of physics and astronomy. A Galileo or Lavoisier or Faraday or Helmholz could found a new science without the aid of expensive instruments.

We shall always have with us the thinkers and the tinkers, those who blaze a trail and lead us to new realms of wonder, and those who patch up matters for a while, but are useful in no finer sense. We shall probably always have men of renown and the mediocre who shine by reflected light. Education will help the slow-witted but it cannot lift them far above their level. Curricula do not make scholars, nor can tutors make wise men out of fools.

The progress of science and of educational facilities during the last hundred years testifies eloquently to the worth of great men. In some measure, too, it has benefited the man of average ability, though he has not been given the chance that he should have. It is not then a point of questioning the importance of education. On the contrary, leaders in the future will wish to vulgarize it more than ever, and do it in a thoroughly democratic manner. Even if much time is wasted in culling the talented from the incompetent, even if the best pupils should suffer from the partialities shown to the dunces, it is better that we raise the general level of intelligence an inch than that of a chosen few a foot.

But on the other hand it must be admitted that schooling has limited functions. The recent multiplication of institutions of learning, of art works and museums, of public libraries and of free lectures for the delectation of curious folk has not brought the results that might have been offhand expected. The response often has been half-hearted and insincere. The fruits have not repaid for the labors of cultivation. The instructor has not found his audience react in a scientific spirit. Education has even spoiled some for lines of work they were naturally fitted for, while many who went without a long drilling in technical subjects have nonetheless emerged out of the struggle for life with a creditable showing, both in earning money and in contributing toward the world's welfare. At all times, it may be said, education has played a less vital part in the development of exceptional personalities than the friends of erudition have liked to confess.

Printing has practically done away with illiteracy, but not with paucity of ideas. Books nowadays are cheap, but thinking is still rare. People have garnered rich stores of fact, but failed to build with them. They have remembered, but not applied knowledge intelligently. Intelligence comes slowly. Intelligence is the power of conquering unforeseen obstacles in theory or practice. Intelligence is the chief weapon of modern times for defense and offense in production. The number of those who have learned to imitate or to understand what was taught at school grows steadily, but the ability to formulate new problems calling for new solutions is always rare.

Yet, because education is so important and leisure a prerequisite to it, socialists rightly insist upon an extension of both. The question thus arises: How shall the additional amount of spare time be used? For rest and entertainment, yes. But also for development of the self and of a social sense. Increasingly the last generation of workers has had spare time for all of these purposes, but past experience does not permit one to hope that the granting in itself of leisure will suffice. The cheapening of consumption goods has sometimes cheapened also our appreciations of art and science. And similarly additional leisure may be abused unless socialism provides the right sort of guidance. One is impressed with the limitations of possession, that is of income, when one watches the way in which people utilize it. To listen to popular music played on the automatic piano, for instance, or to the graphophone is to lose faith in the power of riches. Taste has been little improved, but shallowness is daily encouraged. The magazines still pander to frivolous inclinations and thoughtless readers. The "best seller" is proverbially an inferior piece of literature, and no doubt will remain so. The masses do not frequent our museums, though they have plenty of time for trivialities. The stage does not appeal unless music is reduced to oddities of rhythm and the play made a farce or a melodrama. Everywhere we see tricks of trade prosper, but true art perish.

Up to the present this may have been an inevitable result of our educational system, or of the stigma put upon serious endeavor in pastimes. But if socialism is to elevate social welfare to its noblest heights and give maximum health and intellectual vigor to all, it will have to revise the leisure schedule also. Much teaching in this direction will be needed; much patience and sacrifice on the part of the most highly gifted. Formal schooling will help, but a public supervision of amusements, a fostering of a community spirit for mutual enjoyment and aid will do even more. The socializing functions of play and art have not yet been fully recognized. The charm of enjoying goods in common has not been sufficiently revealed to us because the private property concept has made us suspicious where we should have been open-minded. Leisure may invigorate body and mind, or it may cloy our senses and kill ambition. The habits of the wealthy should be a warning in this respect. They, too, have made less use of their opportunities than seems right. Even among them time drags and ennui is a malady. For lack of natural capacities income and leisure have remained sterile. It has brought no fruit because the inner means of response were not developed.

§ 5. **Income and Happiness.**—What is true of the limits of consumption in developing efficiency and a proper use of consumables is also true of the relation between pleasure and riches. Socialism will not add greatly to happiness, though by objective tests our level of living will be higher. But as remarked before, the objective tests may disagree with the subjective. It is time that people dissociate pleasure from prosperity and judge each by its own indications.

Pleasure as the opposite of pain has of course been eulogized ever since men have breathed and pondered on final values. The cynics of old thought nothing worth while. They belonged to an age in which the old faith was crumbling and the new knowledge was not able to fill an emotional void. When belief in the gods goes and doubt permeates all fields of inquiry a resort to cynicism is natural. Energy must have an outlet somewhere. But it might seem strange that even in modern days philosophers have returned to the calculus of pleasure and pain, were it not that they kept in mind the need of universalizing pleasure, instead of centering it in the individual, and that they reasoned from premises no longer accepted by science. They hoped to make all states of feeling quantitatively measurable so that avoidance of pain became the equivalent of pleasure. They sought to please the largest possible number, and aimed at betterment for that reason, seeing that the masses then had many duties and few privileges.

Hedonism, however, has gone the way of other dogmas. It rendered the eighteenth century a service, since it prepared the way for Enlightenment and the French Revolution, but it no longer meets our requirements because we know that not all feelings can be classified and compared like so many yards of ribbon. The weakness of every subjective norm is its elusiveness. We cannot tell when people are happy. Or if we do dare to, we may be assured quite to the contrary. States of feeling cannot satisfy the student of welfare unless they have an objective correlate, the ratio of the two being more or less definite. But such is not the case.

There are pains akin to pleasure, and states of happiness that bring an undercurrent of chagrin. Just as sick men have been known to work creatively and enjoy life though stricken with agonizing diseases, so trying external conditions have at times been forgotten over the pleasures of work or of buoyant energy. Brief pleasures have brought lasting misery to some, and painful moments have been deliberately courted because they promised enjoyment thereafter. The miser rejoices in the misery of his greed, and the prodigal bemoans his fate while squandering all.

Pleasures cannot be measured by income alone, and if they could be it would not mean anything for science, for socialism, of for social welfare. Happiness is not always the same as pleasure, if by the latter we mean sensations externally stimulated. But for the most part those who are pleased are happy. It is difficult to tell one from the other, unless we arbitrarily consider one a selfish indulgence, and the second an emotion socially sanctioned. But such distinctions are of little import.

The main fact is our inability to create happy states of being at will. We can promote happiness only by popularizing health, wealth, and efficiency. In the long run health means enjoyment. On an average the well-fed and properly clothed suffer less pain than the paupers who have nothing. As a general rule the most intelligent and efficient have sources of happiness not possessed by the helpless.

Yet, whether education and intelligence offer compensations in the way of happiness for the pleasures common among the ignorant is doubtful. Perhaps it would not be too much to say that happiness is essentially an attribute of youth. When we are young and strong, when energy is at a maximum and the power of resisting hardships great, then we enjoy life. Happiness is for those in the early stages of life when the blood flows swift in our veins and the metabolic process quickly replaces waste tissue and poisons. Youth means ignorance and innocence, and both are sources of contentment. Happiness should not be felt, to be real. When we begin to reason about it we probably have lost it. In this sense happiness is youth remembered by old age.

In later life however many sources of happiness arise that childhood is a stranger to. The compensations for toil and duress, for doubt and worries, come in the shape of creative work or of success in conquering a self-imposed difficulty. *Self-measured success is the acme of happiness.* We learn to master ourselves and to help others. There is leadership and a happy home, or friendship and convivialities intellectual or otherwise. There is relaxation and a venting of energy at games. We have the applause of the multitude, and affection for and from others. All these are types of contentment constituting in the aggregate a happy state of life. If the Jeffersonian phrase ever meant anything it must have meant such things, although the thought of rating public welfare by such personal rights and reactions spoiled much of the effect which this creed had upon a later generation.

But if happiness may come so independent of income it clearly may vanish also without regard to income. There are occasions for unhappiness that no one system of production or consumption will remove. Most of our troubles, indeed, come from within. At any rate we may call the environment, in this connection, a constant and declare our feelings variable according to our inborn predispositions. We are annoyed by trifles in personal relations. We chafe at restraints and slights that even the equalization of wealth and ability cannot rid us of. Human traits are such as to make a certain amount of friction unavoidable. We are bound to struggle and suffer in a measure. Comparisons will always be odious, and failure to accomplish what we set out to do will irritate us to the quick. Envy and suspicion, peevishness and false pride embitter the life of many. There is no cure except through gradual adjustment with the aid of education; or perhaps still more so, through breeding according to temperament. Eugenics might in this regard accomplish what economics and socialism must give up as a hopeless task.

Socialism, in fine, can help the masses greatly by economic control since leisure, education, health and efficiency go inseparably together. But it would be folly to expect a millennium of happiness for people simply because we have bettered the objective facts of living. *The aim of the reformer cannot be happiness; it must be achievement and welfare socially measured.* But that is far from ensuring the average man greater bliss consciously felt.

CHAPTER IX

THE LIMITS IN GOVERNMENT

§ 1. The Relation of Empiricism to Political Democracy.— The Communist Manifesto of 1848 concluded with the memorable words: "Workingmen of all the world, unite." It was the final and most stirring appeal of the founders of socialism to the masses whose slavery they hoped to end by a revolution. The nation was not recognized by Marx as the indispensable unit of social life. The fact of the brotherhood of men everywhere was to displace it and make nationalism unnecessary.

Yet it was significant that the fiery words of Engels and Marx were addressed to the international proletariat for a battle against capitalism. The call was not for peace; it was for war on the exploiters who must be subjugated first before the brotherhood of men could become real. Socialism, thus, introduced the idea of cosmopolitanism with a reminder of class struggle, and it expected to establish democracy only by throwing out of the saddle the proud managers of big business. This was a gain and a loss both. It marked an advance over old ideals because the test of democracy was sought in something more important than the right to cast a ballot, and it seemed a step backward because a supposed iron law of wages was to be abrogated by iron force. So the adherents of socialism long interpreted the Manifesto, and with this thought of a revolution quickening the pace of evolution they went to work.

Socialism is a clarion call to action for liberating the

masses. The proof of true socialism is the fraternizing of all men regardless of race or color or nationality, and the extension of the principle of equal rights to all spheres of social activity. Socialism is nothing if not economic democracy internationalized.

What can be said for democracy and internationalism?

The thought of democracy doubtless is as old as history, though the word was not coined till the Greeks learned to reflect on the problems of city government. Aristotle then made his distinctions of types of government and gave reasons for preferring a moderate form of democracy in which the people had a nominal share, but which was really in the hands of a selected few, to monarchy. Democracy as the rule of the people was thus early construed to mean a government *by* the few *for* the many.

It was important, however, that the Greeks were the first to trace the origin of society, for in this way they hit upon the ideal of a state of nature in which all men had been free and equal. The sovereign, they averred, was in those primordial days either the father of the family, or the strongest, most assertive and capable at a crisis. Sovereignty therefore came to signify absolute power, and this has been its main attribute ever since. He is sovereign who has no superior, who exercises his power as he pleases, and who rules by his own initiative, whatever assent expressed or tacit may come from the governed.

The ingenious notion of a compact whereby the freemen living in a state of nature, protected solely by their personal strength and cunning, relinquished their liberties for the sake of ending interminable feuds, added materially to the reputation of Greek philosophy, besides exercising a lasting influence over the development of modern politics. From the seventeenth to the latter part of the eighteenth century nothing seemed so self evident as that people, having been originally endowed by their creator with certain inalienable rights, could have given them up only on terms suitable to themselves, self-protection and the promotion of the social welfare being plainly among the aims of government. It followed from this amplification of an ancient doctrine that the overthrow of the divine right theory of kings was a duty rather than an act of sedition.

The development of natural science strengthened this view of the situation. The founders of physics, astronomy, and biology were men who had little patience with the metaphysical viewpoint. Their concern was the investigation of facts and the establishment of laws by the experimental methods. Where induction was out of the question, the time-honored syllogism did its work, but it was understood that no matter how philosophy might proceed it would start with certain assumptions that begged the ultimate questions professedly answered. In this spirit the empiricists before long became materialists who considered the world a huge mechanism, and somewhat in harmony with this realistic attitude they also treated problems in social life. They favored the utilitarian notion that government is for the governed. They found in the theory of a compact between people and sovereign nothing very objectionable. They were without exception opposed to crass monarchism and took for granted the limitations that gradually were placed upon the Crown.

The idealists in philosophy, on the contrary, stood with the exception of the gentle Spinoza for state-rights, that is to say for the supremacy of the body politic whose head wielded unrestricted powers. Descartes, Leibniz, Wolff,

Kant and Hegel all belonged to this class of thinkers whose tracts on government reflected the absolutistic spirit, not only of their political masters, but also of their own metaphysical doctrines. The difference in this respect between the idealists and empiricists has not been widely noticed or frankly admitted, but the materials for a testing can be easily collected. Broadly speaking one may draw the line of demarcation as suggested: The one group unfailingly championed constitutionalism in practice no less than in theory, the other, namely the metaphysicians, leaned toward political absolutism, even if ostensibly with some reservations in the other direction. But needless to say, the advocates of popular sovereignty had the better of it. Rousseau's notion of the general will of the people won out.

It carried the day first because it fell in logically with the general trend of scientific investigations, and secondly because of the change in economic conditions that is sometimes described by the phrase The Industrial Revolution. This event inevitably favored the laboring classes in that its success presupposed certain individual economic rights, whose counterpart was the principle of universal suffrage and of legislation in accord with public opinion. Autocracy could not hold itself in the face of such changes, though as against this it must be confessed that democracy soon received a setback also.

For it lay in the nature of the new economic situation that the propertied classes held sway over the masses. To be sure, the qualifications for voting or holding a seat in the legislature were soon removed or, as in the United States, never obtained legal recognition. But the enfranchisement was at bottom more nominal than real, since there was as yet no possibility for the poor people to hold office or to swing a vote against the concerted action of the rich industrials and the landed aristocracy. Those who held the purse controlled the government more than ever. The vaunted signs of popular sovereignty proved to be pleasant deceptions that could not compensate the masses for their impotence in the legislative halls. As the decades have rolled by observers have become more and more convinced that something else is needed than the universal ballot to ensure a rule of the people by the people, supposing that such a motto is really recommendable.

As one American writer has recently put it: "Universal suffrage has not given us a democratic industrial system. The enfranchised many have failed to translate their democratic ideals into economic fact."[1] If it is true, as W. Godwin believed in his own day, that "democracy is a system of government according to which every member of society is considered as a man, and nothing more,"[2] then we are not anywhere near our goal, the use of the representative principle of government notwithstanding.

But of course the real question is: How far should government be turned over to the populace, to a plebiscite on public problems, and what is the verdict of social science as to the scope of popular rule?

The pamphleteers of the period of Enlightenment, it is evident, had no appreciation of the real nature of the subject they discussed so glibly now to vindicate absolutism, now to forfend the rights of the citizen. To them man was a finished product of reason chiefly, and society a state designed calculatingly by its members at an early

[1] Hamilton, W. H., "The Price System and Social Policy," in *Journal of Political Economy* for Jan., 1918.

[2] Godwin, W., "Inquiry Concerning Political Justice," Book Five, Chapter 14, where Aristotle's famous definition of democracy is cited with approval.

stage of human development. The historical sense had not yet been cultivated. The perspective was that of the artist who studies a completed picture, rather than that of a traveler who beholds everchanging scenes and new possibilities for investigation. To the absolutists, if government was divinely ordained, harmony between monarch and subject must in the long run prevail. As for the constitutionalist, especially if he accepted the theory of a social contract, a clash of interests could be quickly settled by a resort to arms, but he supposed after all that the contract had been so lucidly drawn up, in full view of the inborn and inalienable rights of man, that an estrangement between the two parties was not to be expected.

But the modern view of the situation cannot be quite so simple.

Manifestly government and people cannot associate so fraternally on a level as the publicists pictured it. Rather, the two will unavoidably, in a certain sense, become strangers for the same reason that boards of directors over a large corporation move in a world different from that of the employees. It is not a question of class privileges or of social stratification, but of specialization in work and interests.

A government becomes a piece of social machinery apart from the general run of people because of the type of men composing it and because of its duties which *eo ipso* imply unique viewpoints. A government, if it functions long enough undisturbedly, will accumulate secrets of trade just as truly as a business concern, and in addition it is bound, in the very nature of its work, to guard important secrets of international relations. Within limits all governments are self-perpetuating bodies, for no change of party or power of ballot can prevent the rise of an elite which, on account of its capacities and experience, tends to keep close to the throne, distributing offices among its members. Government cannot be anything else than a business, if by that term we designate a routine of work and a center of interests relative to which all others appear secondary. The governors must act frequently as though their interests were undeniably the concern of all the governed, even when a difference of opinion might arise at a testing. This is the fundamental fact in the handling of international matters, and on this score the monarchists of old condemned popular sovereignty.

But furthermore, Government ere long means for any nation a set of rules solemnly recorded and carefully preserved. It becomes a code of conduct revered by the people, who are taught to regard nothing more sacred than the laws of the land, even though they challenge science and common sense. Government to many people becomes an institution and a habit, a court of wisdom and a seat of coercive power from which there is no appeal. The average man gives his assent by obeying. That is his way of proving his rights of citizenship unless a special occasion arises.

§ 2. **The Premises of Democracy.**— But in a deeper sense the millions can only be indirect agents of government, not the immediate supervisors of it, as once was believed.

Democracy is an ideal of government essential to the progress of man, but based on assumptions for the most part in conflict with known facts. The value of democracy is therefore not its literal interpretation, but its psychological effect upon people who would do more than they can, who need encouragement the more marked their limitation, and who should have the abstraction of justice on their side no matter how difficult its realization in details,

The premises of democracy are, first, that all people know what is needed for public welfare, second, that all people express their will at the voting booth, and third, that all those elected to office will do the bidding of the people. If we grant these three points we are safe in demanding an unreserved literal exercising of popular sovereignty, but the less faith we have in the postulates the more we shall be inclined to favor a democracy *for* the people by *some,* but not by all, of the people. If the great majority were qualified to pass judgment on political problems, and if, having formed a judicious opinion, they proceeded to express that and nothing else with the understanding that their nominees would carry out to the fullest of their abilities the opinion and wishes recorded in the ballot, then the more truly representative a government would be, the finer the results for all parties concerned. The theory of democracy allows itself considerable license in the premises for the sale of a noble wish!

The obstacles to such unhampered democracy are however many; and they are of a kind calculated to instill much respect.

For as to the first premise we can admittedly not rely on intuitions. What is sound policy for a nation cannot be inferred from scruples of conscience, nor is it to be read from the heavens above. Social phenomena are of all correlations the most complex. We have not yet progressed far in mastering them. We may never feel toward them as the physicist feels about his facts of matter and force or motion. It requires long training and deep attention to seeming trifles to form an opinion of worth on matters sociological. Many facts must be balanced and compared; far more facts than the natural scientist ordinarily reckons with. Hence the uncertainty of some rules in social inquiries, and hence the need of prolonged study for the would be citizen.

But the schooling of the masses has been hitherto unfair to them. It has been faulty for several reasons, one being a one-sided emphasis on subjects remote from our present environment, and a second the exclusion of the great majority from the higher curricula. Education uptodate could never have been adequate to all ideals or needs, for our limits in production unavoidably debarred millions from its blessings. As was shown earlier, if we wish to extend to all children what we now grant ten per cent. of them we shall have to work much harder and greatly improve our methods of work in factory and home. To-day only ten out of each hundred enter high school, and less than two per cent. matriculate for college work. The remainder, the overwhelming majority, is sent to the workbench at the age of fourteen or fifteen, equipped with a scant reading and writing knowledge, but not taught to think closely, to connect cause and effect, to survey a wide gamut of facts, to pierce the shell of things in order to reach a sympathetic understanding of what at first sight may seem gross injustice or a trite detail. We have given the masses the ability to read, but not to comprehend things. We have trained them in the crafts, but not in the sciences nor in the supreme art of living. Their abilities, such as they are, have not been unfolded according to the best prescriptions of the pedagogue. Accurate information is always scarce, but the exclusion of many millions of willing students from the higher branches of learning has made doubly precarious the hold of democracy.

It is acknowledged by one scholar that a true public opinion "can be formed where the bulk of the people are in a position to determine of their own knowledge or by weighing evidence a substantial part of the facts required for a rational decision," but he adds that "knowledge of facts becomes increasingly difficult."[3] A growing complexity of life and widening of economic interests has accentuated the difficulties of old, while our educational system has failed to take due account of them in preparing people for true democracy.

Socialists may of course promise to remedy this defect so that everybody will be able to know what is going on, anxious as well as able to participate actively in politics. One is involuntarily captivated by the prospect of a social order in which all of us get a chance to master the essentials in natural or social science. However, it would be a grievous mistake to bank extravagantly on the possibilities of formal schooling. We may extend educational facilities to a marked degree without obtaining proportionate returns in intelligence. It is not true that a fixed ratio of the one to the other exists. Rather, we all know of types of human beings, some of them bound to succeed in life while others fall by the wayside. Human nature comes in types more or less fixed and regularly recurrent, as the biologist knows. We have the strong and the frail, the clever and the stupid, the imitators and the innovators, the crafty and the naïve, the energetic and the indolent, the courageous and the craven, the stubborn and the docile, and so forth. These classes of people get different results out of the same instructional course. It is not to be supposed that all will benefit by guidance received in the study of social problems, or that, having been informed as to the relevant facts, they will all draw the conclusions most important for the exercise of the rights of citizenship. We may count on many ignora-

[3] Lowell, A. L., "Public Opinion and Popular Government," p. 46.

muses even when science is more conscientiously disseminated. People do not entirely select their data from a social standpoint. Though cognizant of certain facts they will ignore them for the sake of emphasizing their own needs. This is the obstacle mainly interfering with an impartial application of knowledge to practical politics. The masses succumb to emotions when reason alone should govern. The type that acts on analysis is in the minority distinctly, and this type will do the directing whether education has enlightened the populace or not.

The second premise, therefore, loses force also, for just because of the predominance of the strong, calculating, far-seeing minority the great majority seldom remains true to its convictions. Or rather, it receives its ideas from a small group whose word and suggestion superintends the casting of the vote. Social control reigns everywhere. The average man does not spend his time thinking out any particular problem in production or government, but he expects somebody else to give him a problem ready made, much of the solution being already outlined. Under those conditions he will work cheerfully and deliver a product, but not otherwise.

Imitation and suggestion thus become staple devices for learning and for exerting influence. The masses absorb the opinions of leaders as a sponge absorbs water. They fall a prey to suggestibility and follow out commands adroitly administered. From the press or from the pulpit, from the employer and from friends, from the political machine and relatives the most of us get our ideas as to what is right and what we should vote for. The press especially wields an enormous influence over people's minds. It molds opinion more than it passively reflects it, for the brain of the editorial staff is superior to that of the majority, and where the staff is under the control of industrialists or public officials it at any rate still spreads views not primarily developed by the general run of subscribers.

Ward bosses similarly may move us to vote regardless of our personal desires. We listen to them and feel prompted to credit them with superior wisdom. Or we make of political creed a family affair, the son following his father's party, actuated partly by a sense of loyalty or the propriety of things, and partly by the force of habit. Thus we do not ask why certain men are nominated in the convention, or why their names appear on the ballot. We do not go into the history of the candidates, except that the party leaders will consider it somewhat in their proposal for nomination. The wishes of the employer may mean more to us than our private views, for there are avenues that lead to distant goals, and blind alleys that lead us nowhere. Nobody likes to risk much without a chance of gain. Whether it be bribery or promises of advancement, whether it be a mere whim or the innuendos of relatives, whether it be from indifference or because of pressure brought to bear upon men illicitly, men have voted regardless of what they believed, and they will do so again. Few act on decisions painstakingly grounded. Not all are in a position to vote precisely as they please, even if the law protects them. The ballot reflects public opinion, of course, but it originates with a small minority whose powers of perception and of control are plainly in view.

Democracy, thus, is the will of the majority radiating from select groups who, by courting the consent of the masses, succeed in legalizing what once did not need the sanction of law. Political theory, in other words, is far ahead of practice. "No government," wrote Mill in his magnificent essay on Liberty, "by a democracy or a numerical aristocracy, either in its political acts or in the opinions, qualities, and tone of mind which it fosters, ever did or could rise above mediocrity except in so far as the sovereign Many have let themselves be guided, which in their best times they always have done, by the counsels and influence of a more highly gifted and instructed One or Few. The initiative of all wise or noble things comes and must come from individuals; generally at first from some one individual. The honor and glory of the average man is that he is capable of following that initiative—." [4] And in the words of a contemporary writer: "We are governed by minorities just as industries are controlled by them. The problem is not to escape control, but to transform society so that wisdom dominates." [5]

As to the third premise. The people look naturally to leadership, even though at times they are disappointed. They take for granted that their wishes will in the main be honored by the legislator. Yet the pledges for such obedience on the part of men in office are few and indefinite. Party platforms promise much, but are notable for lack of clarity in expression, of precision in the enumeration of particulars. The particulars cannot often be given, for most needs arise *after* men have been installed in office. The barest outline of policies is offered, but one cannot judge from that as to the final interpretation to be put upon them. Either the measures to be acted on cannot be discussed beforehand to any extent, or the thoughts are couched in phrases susceptible of several constructions. Once the governors begin their work the means of checking them up prove strikingly ineffective. There is no way of judging except to obey impulses of the moment. A hostile press may open our eyes,

[4] Mill, J. S., "On Liberty," Chapter 3.
[5] Patten, S. N., "The Reconstruction of Economic Theory," p. 75.

or an honest opponent may point out errors and delinquencies, but beyond that the axiom of responsible ministry is purely nominal. Responsibility is to public opinion, not to wishes registered at the poll. It is to demands agitated among the reigning economic classes, not to principles formulated by science. The latter so far has enjoyed but a passive share in the administration of public affairs.

Whichever way we look at the situation we cannot get away from the limitations inherent in popular control. Democracy always will turn out to be a set of rules by which the minority is permitted, willy nilly, to govern the majority. A few outline the policies, that the multitudes may put the stamp of their approval upon them and thus, by rights of suffrage and representation, become parties to a transaction which few of them really comprehend. The value of political democracy, therefore, is not the equalization of powers of judgment, for that lies far in the future, but the submission *of the mighty, always in theory, and in practice now and then, to the will of the weak.* For the same reasons that a part of our social surplus of goods produced by exceptional talents should go to the normal or deficit producers, the civic rights and duties should be substantially equalized, so each may feel worthy of a place in the social order. To humble the mighty may at times be necessary. The vote and the election campaigns preceding the voting help to fortify the masses against too deep a sense of their own inferiority. What an excess of self-assertion leads to we are told often enough, but immoderate subjection of the Self to class standards is equally reprehensible.

The casting of a vote is symbolic of the power of numbers which the average voter represents. To know that certain offices are legally open to us even when we do not aspire to them is consoling, and a spur to our spirit of enterprise. Democracy politically draped is valuable for these reasons. It puts a premium on social cohesion, on united action by all regardless of differentiations. It harmonizes with our knowledge of human nature. For the lowly are not impotent unless we deny them assistance. The slow-witted need not be a burden until we belittle their ambitions. All of us feel obligations until we are declared irresponsible. The bane of aristocracy is its tendency to declare inert what is quick with life, and to curb development among the mediocre. In a democracy like the socialistic all will have a right to do the unexpected, provided it helps the public at large. It will be for the governors to encourage every effort toward self betterment and to use the data of science so that self and society become one.

§ 3. **Obstacles to Internationalism.**— For a long time to come, however, governments will have to combine science with strategy, for nationalism implies two policies very different in principle. As trustees of the people a government should act honestly, with the regard that one member in a partnership has for the other. But as soon as we scent a conflict of interests between nations we must admit the value of statecraft in a competitive sense.

The scientist should be first of all creative and truthful. Nothing counts but the facts. Service is the keynote of labor, and candor a supreme virtue among collaborators. The government is such an agent of truth and service when it deals with its *own constituency*. But in its dealings with a hostile outside world it must show discretion regardless of rights of duties. It must add the cunning of the fox to the strength of the lion. It must seek to achieve by circumlocution or by a ruse what it could not gain by frankness or amicable advances. Governments are necessarily suspicious of each other as long as they claim sovereignty *amidst radically different conditions for prosperity.* A nation therefore needs two sorts of men and several criteria of conduct; one to govern it at home and the other to guard it against lurking foes. The partnership of truth and falsehood can scarcely be dissolved as long as nationalism prevails and different sovereignties compete for supremacy.

As for the rights of its own citizens a government should subordinate them to the welfare of the great majority. The functions of government, in this respect, will vary with time and place. No one principle can be laid down by which the people are to ensure to themselves utmost personal liberty or a maximum of social striking power.

It is true, as H. Spencer emphasized, that social justice consists in that "every man has freedom to do all that he wills, provided he infringes not the equal freedom of any other man,"[6] but just when the infringement takes place we do not know, except at a given time and place. Similarly, when J. S. Mill observes that "the only part of the conduct of any one for which he is amenable to society is that which concerns others"[7] we will agree offhand. But how shall we determine what actions are of social import, and which concern solely the individual? The proper sphere of government is not found as easily as was thought by the Manchestrians. We have abandoned the theorem that government is an evil and self-expression naturally a virtue. We have individually perhaps held control to be a sad duty, a necessary evil,

6 Spencer, H., "Ethics," Part Four, Justice, Chapter 6, No. 27.
7 Mill, J. S., "On Liberty," Introductory.

but at the same time we have found out that liberty is not so much a reservation of rights to say and do things as one of duties by the observance of which the largest possible number of people in a given area can master the complexity of civilization.

The history of American ideals of democracy is an instructive example of this relativity of freedom. Paternalism was once decried as something un-American, as smacking of monarchy. But increasingly as the western frontier has disappeared, as city life has encroached on the country side, as density of population has increased and our economic organization has expanded and become more intricate, increasingly in about the same measure we have added to our functions of federal and local government, until to-day warnings to do and not to do certain things greet us on all sides. Laws have been passed on behalf of the citizen which two generations ago would have seemed as ridiculous as indeed they would have been inappropriate. What twenty million agriculturally engaged Americans considered good government is one thing, and what a seething mass of urbanites without land, huddled together like sheep in a pen, deem adequate government is quite another thing. It would not be an exaggeration to say that functions of government grow in proportion to density of population and to per capita production of goods.

Democracy certainly must anticipate dark days when social relations become too interlaced; for it may mean that social stratification is sanctioned and the antagonism of economic groups openly recognized. It is when this stage of structural development has been reached that international relations, too, assume a sinister aspect. The functions of government will then proclaim a new norm of individualism, one that would outrage the individualistic sense of the primitive man, say of the colonist in Jacksonian days.

The prerogatives of sovereignty, however, are most fully invoked in international relations. It is here that the individual is nothing and the state everything. The government acts on behalf of all its citizens against the presumption of outsiders. It speaks as though the citizens were temporarily a means to an end, the end being the promotion of interests as understood by the governors. Minority rule is then most in evidence. Leadership and might carry the day. The weal and woe of untold millions rests in the hands of a very few men steering the ship of state. The principle of competition holds sway, and nations match their rights as they ordinarily match their goods in a search for markets.

The nation is not presumably as old as the race or tribal unit. It depends upon our definitions of both. But there is ample evidence to show that blood ties have never limited the expansion of groups. Whatever race characteristics may be, peoples of different physical make-up of different languages and literatures, have been united under one common rule and fought shoulder to shoulder against their own kinsmen as well as against aliens. The nation has always proven to be a union of individuals welded by exceptional leadership. Leaders of men have fought each other, and external circumstances have prompted people to side with one or the other. Groups have been made strong by a minority which, taking upon itself the onus of battle and vigilance, was given the control of internal affairs no less than of warfare.

A nation is the product of force. Leadership has made it. Sovereignty is the absolute right of leaders to safeguard their nation against the attacks of rival nations.

Such were the original attributes of the sovereign, alongside of which the rights of jurisdiction and of taxation developed early. A nation may not be economically self-sufficient. It rarely has been. But it always represents an organization of fighters who will place their own welfare above that of any outsider. This is a rule the exceptions to which are few and far between.

The more advanced our methods of production the larger a nation may grow, for plainly it requires either physical force or solidarity of interests to govern millions from a single center. The Ancients, and notably the Romans, succeeded in building vast empires covering millions of square miles because their organization of fighters had no equal. On the other hand, nations may become strong numerically if they are able to find enough food on a small area, or to purchase it with finished products. This was commonly the case since the discovery of new continents, with immense natural resources awaiting exploitation, has furnished European nations a welcome outlet for manufactures. Race ideals have always been an impediment to aggressive nations, but not an invincible one. Differences in language and intellectual traditions, in religion and in physical traits such as color and stature have tended to keep people apart. Yet these natural barriers have not always prevented a conqueror from gathering under his scepter a mighty host of subjects.

What must determine the size of nations is chiefly technical means of communication, travel, and transportation, methods of production, the disposition of natural resources, and principles of government. As long as topographical conditions vary greatly, as long as mountains and water could separate people by making travel impossible, as long as sparsity of resources kept people poor and widely scattered, so long the agglomeration of many millions under a single flag was out of the question. And for precisely these reasons nationality will be a dominant factor for centuries to come.

There will never be enough time and wealth to permit migration at regular intervals for the exchange of interests, thoughts, and manners. Physiographic differences are bound to differentiate peoples in different continents, or even within one continent. The historical background of the ancient world is so much a part of its modern inhabitants that they can never hope to rid themselves entirely of its fatal effects for purposes of internationalism. There is no promise of an amalgamation of races or of nationalized groups. The socialists admit this, and others assume it is a matter of course.

If socialism then speaks of cosmopolitanism it cannot be with the desire to abrogate nationalism, but only to the end that a better understanding between the several sovereign units may be attained. Socialism is eager to *fund sentiments*, as it has professed great faith in the funding of *goods*. The most ardent of socialists would abridge sovereign rights so as to make individual nations amenable to an international tribunal representing the whole world. The underlying thought is the liberation of the masses from the yoke of capitalism, but the incidental feature is the abolition of wars. Socialism pins its faith in the goodness of human nature as found in the average man. It places the responsibility for class struggle and international strife with the magnates of business, confident that a reorganization of the industrial system would disarm them and free mankind from a horrible incubus. Socialism wishes to limit sovereignty, but not the duties of government. In this respect its aims are diametrically opposed to those of Laissez Faire and of competitive capitalism, which stress the need of nationalism as over and against the rights of the individual within each nation. The issue is clearly defined.

But in order to agree to the limits of socialistic government we must first distinguish between superficial and basic causes of war. Lack of communication cannot explain them, for in the very century that the means of communication and travel were most perfected, intelligence being flashed across continents and oceans with lightning speed, wars have been as common as ever, besides being conducted on a much larger scale. Nor is the type of government apparently a decisive factor, considering that democracies have fought as lustily as autocracies. The overthrow of absolutism did not spare France or England any wars. Neither have the South American republics or the United States escaped them entirely, though thanks to their youth, perhaps, and to their remoteness from the centers of trade they suffered less than the Europeans.

And in the third place it would be folly to attribute wars to economic pressure if that is to mean lack of food or of the necessaries of life as the masses know them. Wars have been as plentiful in the days of cavedwellers as to-day. Density of population has not multiplied them, nor has the modern abundance of necessities made them impossible. Regardless of an abundance of supplies nations have entered upon costly wars; regardless of needs, measurable by individual standards, governments have declared themselves constrained to levy armies either in self defense, or on behalf of third parties.

Hence the meaning of the indisputable fact that wars must be traced to economic pressure is somewhat different from the one commonly accepted. It has to do not only with the "economic man" that economics has so often alluded to, but likewise with types of men and their rôle in social growth.

The economic man is a product of evolution. The universal surplus of seed coupled with the scarcity of foods brought about a struggle in which pugnacity and acquisitiveness became invaluable assets. Those who would or could not fight to acquire a subsistence were inevitably killed off. The instinct of self-preservation could express itself in no other way than in willingness and ability to fight for the biologically essential things. The sex struggle was an accompaniment of the contest for self-preservation, the two being inseparably connected.

The course of history points to the effect of economic conditions upon the development of social norms, but the innate faculties of man were in turn the means for enlarging the economic environment. Thus the selfish instincts eventually aided in the arousal of a group consciousness almost as strong as parental love and sex passion. The original need of food ceased to preoccupy men. They specialized more and more for the accumulation of non-necessities which their imagination made desirable, and the possession of which meant power. That is to say, since strength like everything else is relative, the means to survival were not simply an abundance of food, but all those instruments by which an enemy could be subjugated in a battle. Not the mere muscular strength, but ax and arrow, sword and scimitar became important, and again not weapons but means of defense, like walls and citadels, moats and armor, decided the issue. And later on subtler devices warded off the foe. The power of body was dwarfed by the force of explosives. Armor plate, instead of shielding the knights, was used to clad ships and fortresses. Industry supplied the government with weapons vastly superior to anything the primitive man had known, but the victory still went to those who relatively excelled in men and arms. Iron and coal and chemistry and Kartells came to count as much in an international struggle as personal strength and nimbleness for prehistoric tribes.

The economic man cultivated his powers of reasoning, but he could not divest himself of reflex actions and instincts bred in countless ages of ferocious combat with animals and fellowmen. The test for superiority changed, but the instincts remained the same. Instead of foods the desideratum became a surplus of capital goods with which to produce enjoyable consumption goods in times of peace, and weapons of defense in times of war. In his eagerness to acquire creative comforts our ingenious man also advanced the methods of warfare. His prosperity which once turned on the sufficiency of food and clothing now varied with his possession of a large stock of raw materials and finished articles.

The social group expanded, but leadership became more precarious. Individual might had to be buttressed more and more by the approval of rival companions. Prestige hinged on wealth because everybody valued wealth for its own sake, besides desiring it as token of providential favor or of unusual ability, of privilege and power. Wealth meant leisure in peace, and victory in war. The control of riches in land or in capital enabled man to command respect and obedience where the weight of personality alone might not have sufficed. The economic man, in this sense, is an imperishable product of evolution and progress, a fact all science and sentiment must take into account. While wealth has its uses in war it will be doubly valuable also in days of peace.

But the accumulation of wealth rests largely with exceptional men. The inventors and managers of capital, the organizers of men for productive purposes, and the proprietors of natural resources — these form the nucleus from which social growth must be deduced, just as premises give rise to a conclusion. The correlations of social phenomena are many, and what is cause or effect may never be completely determinable. Yet it is certain that without the right sort of natural resources and right leadership for production or public control nothing great can be achieved. The place of one nation among others varies with the use of resources in material and men made by the small minority now dominating business. When a nation boasts many great leaders it is likely to grow rapidly, to increase its population by selling manufactures for foodstuffs, to raise its level of living, to widen its horizon of thought and politics, and to search the world for greater riches.

If physical barriers do not forbid, an aggressive attitude toward outsiders is thus sure to find approval. The leaders want power and empire, the masses demand comforts and glory, i. e., such glory as the fear of rivals or the consciousness of past triumphs may bring. War, in brief, is a *means of equilibrating differentials of power between nations who rank as sovereign units, but whose real might is lodged in the hands of a few who by virtue of office or of inborn superiorities decide the fate of the multitudes.* It is hardly an error to call the leaders the creators and destroyers of life, in that their sagacity and energy alone provides the means to an increase of population. But their struggle for shining supremacy also engulfs the masses periodically in bloody wars, wars that decimate the population and redistribute sovereign powers so that another period of growth for somebody may follow.

Differentials of national power will always exist because inventions change the value of natural resources. What at one time means little, may be highly prized and coveted at another. In ancient days soil fertility was a prime asset. To-day coal and iron stand out prominently. During the later middle ages commerce with the far east helped nations to a lordly position. A century hence maritime facilities may be less significant than circumstances favoring aërial navigation. Just now oil and copper are items of maximum valuation, but there is no gainsaying that countries now obscure and despised for their backwardness may rise to eminence because of discoveries yet to be made by now leading civilizations. The notion of a balance of power dates from days when two or three nations were the arbiters of Europe, but it is doubtful whether it will ever mean anything else than the division of power among a few, whose policy is law for all others.

No nation is as yet ready to renounce its sovereign rights. All nations have reserved for themselves the right of autonomy in internal affairs, even if elsewhere they had nothing to say. The spirit of nationalism is rampant these days. It has been fed and fêted by the latest war, instead of being restrained by it. Even now nations are preparing for rehabilitation commercially, for the expansion of business at the other's expense, for the delimitation of spheres of influence. Investments and colonies, mandates and protectorates, alliances and tariff conventions figure prominently in the daily press. Sovereignty is still regarded as absolute and inviolable. What kings once claimed is now fitly ascribed to the people, but if nationalism is to continue on competitive lines natural differences will not only be accentuated, but the motto of particularism will estrange nations so that arbitration of clashing claims becomes difficult.

Human nature gives us no ground for expecting perpetual peace by the introduction of the plebiscite or of female suffrage. Women at all times have supported men in a combat. The sex relation is so entirely mutual that it is folly to expect from women what men cannot do. The passions of the multitude are easily aroused to ungovernable fury. Nothing appeals like an argumentum ad hominem. If the leading classes give moral support to a martial government it is sure to find a vent. Patriotism covers a multitude of sins. Nationalism is a growth that thrives on secrecy and on centralization of powers. What is a domestic question and what a justiciable case, what an attribute of sovereignty and what a question for adjudication? What are the obligations of a protectorate and what the limits of armament internationally permitted? These are problems not to be solved with science or law, but with combats or concessions.

Socialism has a hard road to travel in many respects, but it is particularly embarrassed in its attempts at internationalism and enduring — we won't say perpetual — peace. The safest preventives at its disposal are education and publicity, decentralization of economic powers, and a leveling of incomes. If by equalization of opportunities and economic rights we can teach the average man to think; if in the wake of enlightenment morality will gradually subordinate feelings of race and nationality to the concept of humanity; if in giving the masses an active share in government we can banish camarillas of Machiavellianism, bringing into the light of day the precise facts at issue — then we may hope to chain grim Mars and smooth the path for Peace. But socialism has not yet declared itself willing or able to redistribute the world's goods irrespective of national boundaries; nor are the means near at hand that make such an equalization of resources and policies possible. Tried in only one or two countries socialism might meet the fate of bi-metallism which could not hold itself in the midst of gold standards.

To conclude. The weaker system of production, if international trade is to follow competitive principles, is assuredly the socialistic. Costs can be lowered if we have no conscience. Markets may be conquered at the sacrifice of millions at home, provided the law does not interfere. Socialism will value personality above product. It may raise the social dividend without cheapening particular types of goods fit for exportation. It might be compelled to buy imports at prices costly to the consumer. In rich countries socialism will tend to lower levels of living if it wishes to aid poorer countries. The gain will come some day, if all coöperate on one principle, but for the present the outlook for internationalism is disquieting. The limits of government point to nationalism in spite of its perils, in spite of grievous experiences in the past.

CHAPTER X

A PETITION

§ 1. Foundations in Social Science Restated.— What has so far been said should now enable us to summarize as follows:

Social reform manifestly must be based on social science. The physician in this respect sets a good example to the socialist and to other prophets of a better world. He does not suggest cures until he has analyzed his case. Diagnosis and prognosis go together. What is more, a careful record of the course of the malady is kept, and only in the light of past experiences, which are compared with the individual case, is treatment offered. The physician relies upon the facts of physiology and allied sciences for his power of aiding the sick.

The would-be healer of social ills can do no better than look to the foundations of social processes before going to work. The data of biology and psychology, of sociology and of economics furnish the light by which eventually a prescription may be filled for the curing of social patients. The diagnosis may not be perfect. The symptoms may mislead us. The issue of the disease may be most unexpected. But in spite of the limitations to which all science is subject, and which the reformer must bear in mind, his plans have a chance of success only in so far as they square with actualities. Whether we are dealing with a political platform, or with a petition of rights for the people, each must be based on facts, and accept the restraints which facts impose.

For purposes of reform as well as for research in general the empirical standpoint alone can satisfy. There is no gain in postulating sources of truth which lie beyond the ken of our senses. To predicate innate ideas about anything is useless, for the predication itself is not innate, and if it were it could not change the nature of our knowing. The distinction between things and things-in-themselves is entirely gratuitous. It is useless except to call our attention to the sources of our knowledge and to the methods we employ in reasoning.

There is no way of learning except by our power of sensing things, by our ability to respond selectively to, and to remember, the stimuli acting from without and from within. Our senses furnish the basis for knowledge. The data of our consciousness and its reactions measure the scope of our learning. We receive stimulations and respond in certain ways. We remember and construct associations which according to purpose and setting terminate in action, or perhaps do not.

The outside world is one of regularities because of our ability to perceive, select, and remember. Associations alone make possible the connections by which we bring order into chaos. It is through inference by enumeration and by comparison of resemblances and differences that we obtain classes of things and laws of nature. The laws that science speaks of are sequences and coexistences recurring with different degrees of regularity. We can control them in a measure. We can modify some of the laws, but only by changing ourselves. Everything for that matter is subject to change. Nothing is absolutely rigid or definitive. The groups of events which we bind together and experience as correlatives or laws change in scope and contents. As students we add to, and subtract from, such facts involved in a given situation according to time and circumstance. From time to time all our knowledge must be restated. Its values have undergone a change without our at first being conscious of it. Thus sciences grow, and in this sense all sciences are interrelated, the boundary lines shifting and becoming clear and blurred by turns.

But our knowledge is also relative in this respect that not all people judge facts alike. They have many characteristics in common, but in different degrees. Our anatomy, for instance, is substantially the same for all. In instincts tending to survival we are much alike. Our sense perceptions in general correspond so that we all see or hear the objects or noises about us. But increasingly, as we move away from the most fundamental traits of human nature, we notice differences in men, in their interests and methods of valuation. The number and the significance of factors in a given situation appear differently to different people. The events may be called variables whose functioning is the subject of science. The fact of interrelation is observed by all, and will be agreed to from the start, but its nature or functioning challenges the acumen of the ablest, indeed cannot often be established indisputably.

The variables of events, or experiences that fill our life and become the special concern of scientists, are all either causes or effects according to viewpoint and needs of the moment. It is not that the two are generically distinct, but that some factors in a situation are considered as constants, relative to which all others are treated as variables. We understand things by cross reference. We explain the obscure by comparing it with the clear, or what seems clear. We select our subjects for observation, and by focussing our attention upon particulars get the truth which at the time is sought. Purposes and circumstances govern all our searches for law in nature and for rule in personal conduct or social policy.

It follows then that sciences are not only interconnected, but also that for all sciences there is but one method. The man on the street who is not specially trained will yet, in the main, use the modes of reasoning employed by the professional student. The two stand in this respect on a level because both are products of one course of evolution. Just as man is a unit and therefore all social phenomena interrelated, so scientific and unscientific methods of thinking have much in common. The chief difference between the untutored man and the scientist is the latter's enlarged fund of associations which permits him to extend greatly his comparisons and test thoroughly his inferences by enumeration and analogy. He practices a more careful selection of data, makes exacter measurements thanks to the use of instruments not possessed by the layman, and hence, as final result, boasts a wider scope of investigation and of generalization. The scientist stands on a higher plane because he excels in association and measurement. The scientist does not allow himself to be hindered by irrelevant premises. He assumes only the will to live. That given, his world of experience and truth is mechanistically pictured or at any rate understood.

Science is necessarily mechanistic. But this does not prevent it from accepting that viewpoint as correct which makes man appear self-directing and responsible according to socially instituted standards. The notion of freewill is no impediment to the scientist. He may grant it, and then pursue his studies as though it did not exist. *Freewill is a way of looking at the outside world from within.* It is an egotistic norm of valuation. It enables us to refer events to ourselves, or one part of a situation to another. In social sciences notably the assumption of a freewill is a prospective way of viewing plans of action, i. e., coming events. There is no objection to considering each man the maker of his own fortune, as though he were lord over his Self and the fashioner of his destinies. But statistics show that events, though supposedly willed, happen with considerable regularity, and that what a man really does is far different from the things he believes he could do if necessary. A belief in illimitable will is usually a picturing of possibilities with the aid of the imagination. Associations outstrip action!

Similarly science does not conflict with ethics or religion. The latter two may be deemed independent fields for investigation if it's found profitable, but the evidence of natural and social sciences favors the subordination of moral norms to the general scheme of consciousness and sociation. What we think right, and what we wish of an unknown future, these are facts that are an integral part of our whole being. There is no method for understanding the Ought and the Soul except by analyzing self and society as the scientist is wont to.

If we apply some of these fundamentals to social science we shall find at once the limits of all social movements and of all reform schemes. No one can work without the right basis for physical reactions. No one can excogitate a world entirely apart from his surroundings. No one will propose betterments, except he is bound by the traditions back of him and by the shortcomings of science as they exist at his time. All social events are conceived as knit together. The relations are intimate or remote, but they may be proven to exist if we trace events far enough. Yet for the same reason all truths are relative to time, place, and circumstance, or to put it more accurately, to place, period, and people. It is the environment in general and particular, it is the epoch of social development or of national growth, it is the group experiencing the events, be it large or small — it is in the midst of these facts that all social principles find their bounds. There are too many variables to permit an exhaustive interpretation. There are many events functioning as variables, because human nature is so much more complex than either animal or plant, or than any of the relations of the inorganic world.

On the other hand, the main facts of human nature are definitely ascertainable and virtually immutable. The changes in man come so slowly that we can scarcely perceive them. To ourselves we are the constant by reference to which the events about us appear as variables which, more or less completely, we may control. Human nature is practically a constant, though per individual the force of variation is as great as that of heredity is self evident.

Precisely because of this substantial definiteness of our make-up the data of psychology and of biology furnish us a clue to standards of prosperity. A theory of prosperity depends on the knowledge of those two sciences. The principles of sociology and of economics are the last auxiliaries toward a science of social welfare which politics should apply. But the social sciences cannot go ahead until the more fundamental inquiries have attained a certain mastery of facts. Psychology, because it studies the individual, serves to clarify our notions of reasoning, and because it is basic to social studies, it may serve also to help formulate our norms of right and wrong. Right and wrong are criteria of social origin whose individual aspects are treated by psychology.

Without the combined action of natural and social science, then, we cannot hope to arrive at clear ideas of prosperity or of reform. Socialism was among the first movements for betterment to recognize this cardinal fact. Hence, if for no other reason, it deserves a conspicuous place in the history of human thought. But, indeed, socialism has a mission for other reasons still. It is not only the logical continuation of doctrines first enunciated by Comte the Positivist and Mill the Utilitarian, but in addition it broached for the first time in unmistakable tones the relation of economics to non-economics, or, as we might say, of wealth to weal.

§ 2. **Errors in Socialism.**— Socialists committed mistakes in action, and they espoused for a long time (in part still espouse) teachings not tenable in the light of current science. Socialism, for instance, was wrong in promising to eliminate all maladjustment and give to men a millennium. It was wrong in declaring conditions of production and of exchange to be causative of all other facts of sociation, as though one was the maker of the other. It will not help us, as we have seen, to trace a chain of events in one direction only. The relation of events would be warped. It is not a question of economic man building all the rest in man, but one of lines of thought and action radiating from one center. Man is a single whole, and all life's experiences must be interlaced as a result of it. Without this conception life becomes a mystery, or else a mere catalogue of facts as meaningless as the variegation of a kaleidoscope.

Socialism furthermore erred in attributing all values to one factor, and particularly in comparing effort-in-time with the market values of a competitive régime. Prices are not measured by labor except in a very general way, and what is more important: Prices cannot in this way be identified with incomes. Socialism, by the same token, failed in trying to correlate prices of goods with personal incomes, or even with factorial incomes. We can sometimes impute values to each one of many elements contributing toward a single product. The physicist does it, and other sciences may do the same. But in the realm of exchange the imputation is indirect and can lead to no nice measurements. To declare labor an essential in production is one thing, and to measure wants by work is another thing. The socialist aimed at the wrong thing, to begin with, when he proposed to explain incomes by prices, and he failed again because, having set his target, he did not aim well.

The founders of socialism similarly erred in expecting everything good from the abolition of capitalism, for private ownership of the means of production and of exchange does not explain all evils. They were proven false prophets also by future events, for misery, while it has perhaps not abated a great deal, has certainly not increased to the degree that was apprehended. The Marxian theory of misery contains an element of truth, but it can be found only in Marx's "Economic Interpretation of History," and there it is marred by the fond belief that nationalization of capital would remove all evils.

Lastly, socialists laid themselves open to charges when they promised the world a much higher level of living than is now assured to the bulk of the people. They expect a gain in productiveness, thanks to the abolition of private capitalism, which cannot be logically deduced from the facts of population and environment, nor agrees with socialistic ideals of self development. The limits in race improvement are also much in evidence, whether we appeal to our own powers of observation or to the verdict of science. Everywhere we find bounds prescribed that socialism has often overlooked, or promised to set at nought by the application of one general principle, to wit the abolition of private property. But such optimism is never fruitful. It can only prompt some people to misunderstand the nature of democracy and to look forward to change such as science knows nothing of. Democracy is more than a distributive norm, and less than a complete equalization of governors and the governed. The same differences among men that prevent us from fixing a ratio between property and personality, or between economic income and psychic outgo, also point to limits in government, no matter how liberally we scatter rights of voting and of office holding.

§ 3. Merits in the Viewpoint of Socialism.— Socialism, then, may be criticized from many standpoints, since its premises and conclusions partly belong to a period which science has left far behind. But as against these blanks we must note, too, the winning numbers in the game. The founders of socialism have conferred great benefits upon us, because they were exceptional men who saw far and gathered wisdom from many founts. It would be strange if they had not discovered new truths in all their quest for betterment, or failed to enhance the value of old truths. Men like Marx and Engels or Lassalle will always prove a boon to society, for any determined defense of scientific endeavor leads to moral as well as to intellectual regeneration.

Socialism was right in adopting an empirical position, in emancipating itself from all hankerings for a transcendental universe. Socialists were among the first to preach relativism and to apply the principle of instability to human history. The evolution of our thoughts and actions was shown to be a law pervading our whole social development. The dual aspect of eternal truth was revealed sharply. Thus dogmatism was dealt a severe blow, the absolutism of Hegel becoming a brief on behalf of the masses.

Socialism is right in correlating science and reform: It was the earliest of the great movements for reform on a purely scientific basis. True, to divorce science from sentiment is not always possible, nor will all agree to its being a lofty ideal. It is much the same thing when art and morality are coupled. Some object, and others applaud. But it is important for the reformer that he curb his desires in accordance with scientifically established limits, and this the socialists sought first to do. They hoped for betterment through the workings of a cosmic law. They argued for sweeping changes and at times took refuge in rebellion and hyperboles of speech. But on the other hand they did not demand redress merely because their conscience drove them, or because somebody urged them to protect the weak. The chief principle from the outset was the connecting of revolution with evolution.

This likewise enabled the founders of socialism to incorporate ethics with economics. The socialistic theory of prosperity harmonizes with modern science in that it insists upon verification. The proof of conduct is held superior to protestations of creed. Whenever this is done, whenever service is placed above suffering the road is opened for progress. By objective tests the good and the bad should be defined. This socialism has aimed to do from the start. Ethics was recognized as part of social science. The empirical, or if you will, the pragmatic viewpoint was thus given a specific meaning that all could understand and criticize as they pleased.

The socialization of religion is a by-product of this mode of reasoning. Socialists have always championed the Golden Rule as the quintessence of holy communion. They have stood by those who brought religion to earth and gave it a social mission. That ideals are of the earth and yet may rise above the earthy, this is the stand taken by the positivists, and this attitude socialism has consistently supported.

But socialism was also right in stressing the social roots of evil. The older thought that man fell from grace or that nature was to blame if people lived in pain and poverty was calculated to encourage pessimism. It drove men to despair and granted an easy sinecure to privileged classes. Compared to this soothing sirup the socialistic medicine had real merit and promised a cure. It agreed with the gospel of prosperity which science now is interested in, and called attention to the predominance of the instincts over our habits of reasoning. That man was first an animal and next a being of reason was always admitted by socialists. The economic interpretation means partly this. But it also hints at the possibilities for self development. Reason enthroned is as true a symbol for socialism as the tiger stalking for prey. The balancing of primordial selfishness with socialized altruism, this is the task of the future, and to this task socialists have ever bent their energy.

Socialism is not averse to recognizing the beast in man. The veneer of civilization fools least of all the socialist. But for all that he has declined to subscribe to the teachings of competitive economics. The founders of socialism were pioneers in social science and advanced critics of the classical system which made a fetich of individualism. They did well in exposing the logical consequences of Ricardianism, and they made some contributions to the critique of marginal economics which until recently held almost undisputed sway. A stress on collectivism may lead to extravagant expectations. An exclusive reliance on state ownership will disappoint its sincerest friends. But that evils exist and reforms are needed no one will deny. Yet it was socialism which first systematized the business of meliorism and opened our eyes to the significance of private property. To take nothing for granted is a sound maxim in science. Socialists learned it early. They did not take private property, e. g., for granted. We can do no better than follow in their footsteps and search into the grounds of an institution which exercises such an incalculable influence over our weal and woe.

§ 4. **Existing Evils in Our Economic System.**— Reform undoubtedly is needed. Evils exist in plenty, and not all of them are necessary even at this stage of social development. We may agree to the old saw that nothing is perfect and yet apply ourselves with zest to the task of bettering socio-economic conditions.

The evils are known to all and need no lengthy discussion. We have among us the diseased and the cripples, the subnormal in mind and the totally disabled. We have criminals of many types and vice that goes unpunished by law. There is cruel hunger that cannot be stilled, and pauperism no philanthropist can root out. Some overwork or suffer from the effects of excessive specialization. Others again are treated unfairly in a personal way and resent the insults thrust at them. We know of many who are kept unfit for civic duties, who cannot be made desirable members of a democratically governed country. Class struggle is real, and discontent widespread.

All these evils have existed for centuries and in part cannot be removed. It is not possible for instance to ensure everybody good health by safeguarding him when at work, or by scientific sanitary engineering. Gluttony and bad habits are as common a source of illness as accidents or bad housing conditions. The congenitally disfigured and disabled we shall perhaps have always with us, for the problems of genetics have not yet suggested ways and means for controlling natural variations. The blind and the deaf and dumb are a burden that society must shoulder with resignation. The demented or the moron, that aristocrat of the feeble-minded, may be helped by trained guardians, but they will for long times to come form a certain percentage of our population. And so with the rest of the shortcomings. Not all crime is traceable to social surroundings. There is some evidence to show that born criminals exist, and that vicious habits may be inherited as well as acquired in unobtrusive ways.

Among the rich, too, there is much profligacy and barrenness, both of the physical and the intellectual kind. Money rules not uncommonly at the expense of mentality and manhood. The reign of money is plutocracy, whose undesirable features have been sufficiently explained. Even in a political democracy the money-king has some power. And power breeds arrogance, and arrogance leads to friction and class consciousness. Idleness is the fruit of wealth as well as of inherited lethargy. Too many nowadays prosper in languor, supinely enjoying ill-gotten gains. Complacency and egoism flourish among the rich who control a large portion of the national income. Extreme concentration of income is as obnoxious from the standpoint of comradeship and solidarity of interests as it may seem unjust to the defenders of a high material level of living. It is in the competitive régime as heretofore prevailing that unearned increments enrich the one, while hard laborers are rewarded insufficiently. The unearned portion crops out at all sorts of places. We see it in the appreciations of natural resources, of real estate, in the winnings of the profiteer and stock broker, in the scoop made by the keeper of roulette tables, in rentals squeezed out of the toiler's weekly pittance, in usury rates levied by the small capitalist, in the collection of royalties and patent rights, in gifts and briberies received by young and old, with or without their understanding of the evils involved.

A further result of past competitive practices has been an absurd valuation of goods and a disproportionate output of luxuries, considering the needs of the great majority. The lawyer, for instance, who helps his client in the criminal circumvention of the statutes enacted in defense of the consumer is repaid richly for his effort. A princely retainer-fee perhaps is his share of the bargain. He has, for his purposes, made good use of his position. Pandects and precedents at court have to him been not merely a mine of information, but also of gold which many others, covetous of success, will envy him. The farmer on the contrary, who with his toil produces the essentials wherewith to feed his nation, is fortunate if he makes a living. Indeed, not infrequently he had less than a standard wage. Again, trivial personal services rendered to the wealthy bring a magnificent largess, while the most deserving must get along in beggarly fashion. The businessman knows how to cater to the rich and glean from their table many a crumb. The lowly are naturally inclined to make the most of an anomalous situation. They cannot change the economic order, so the best thing is servile adaptation, a regard for the wishes of those that have, so they themselves may pocket some gains. For ridiculous services exorbitant prices, and with the price a shower of tips even more generous!

Gross inequality in the distribution of incomes has thus led to pompous displays on the one hand, and to sad wants on the other. The contrasts of rich and poor evoke dismay and wonder. It is what the masses do not get rather than what the opulent display that impresses one. One sees what progress so far has not accomplished. Crowded and filthy tenements not only repel those of cleanly habits, they also are an indictment for those who by their extravagances turn labor into wrong channels. The regalia of West End cannot make us forget the ragamuffins of East End. The fascinations of Fifth Avenue relieve in no wise the squalor a few blocks away. Slums are an evil, whether we live in them ourselves or not.

The time for a thorough study of social processes is now. Now is the time to think and act on matters sociological. These are the days when reform must interest alert men and women. The European upheaval is an instance both of evils fatally ignored and of experiments in social regeneration. Circumstances alter cases. A readjustment to conditions precipitated by the war is impending. Whether all of the changes now advocated will meet the test of time no one can tell, but that betterments are under way should be manifest to all. The Old World is rapidly becoming a new world.

The United States, too, is in a favorable position for a retesting of social norms. It represents the largest block of natural resources ever placed under one flag. No other belt on this globe of ours equals it in richness or in the efficiency of its population. We have minerals and water-power, timber lands and vast plains yielding bountiful harvests. We have untold wealth aiding us in production, a high level of living that may still be raised higher by right methods, and a stock of people whose full capacities have not yet been put to a trial. With so much to act on, with such assets to manage for the best of all, the cause of social science should not be deserted. A disinterested but wholehearted application of knowledge can nowhere bring richer rewards.

The socialist addresses himself in this spirit to all classes of people. Not merely to the professional student or to statesmen, but to all workers, and in particular to the average wage earner who has most at stake in this movement for a redress of wrongs. Without definite knowledge nothing can be achieved. Without the goodwill of the majority no public action can be taken. Without enthusiasm no sustained effort is likely. But if in the future the average man applies himself diligently to problems of social welfare extraordinary achievements are in store for us.

§ 5. **A Petition.**— A petition for redress of existing evils rests on this assumption. It takes for granted that the data of social science are duly consulted, and that only a joint effort of all can net lasting benefits. This is the characteristic of a theory of prosperity weaned from the conceits of bygone centuries.

The socialist, and with him the student of social processes, pleads for equalization of rights and duties everywhere so far as the norms of maximum welfare permit. We must equalize — that is make less uneven — the distribution of income by virtual, if not actual, abolition of the right of inheritance, by taxation, and by increasing the public ownership of industrial plants and of natural resources. Inheritance, as J. S. Mill acknowledged in his "Principles of Political Economy," is no logical adjunct of private property. Its praiseworthy features are few, but its demerits stand out boldly.

Taxes also may be revised so as to conform to a collectivistic rather than to an individualistic standard. In the past the faculty theory of taxation took for granted what socialism denied. Tax rates were meant to rectify errors of ruthless competition, but the roots of the evil were not thereby disturbed. To tax the financially able means to define ability to *earn* as well as ability to pay taxes. This is the consideration which should govern us from now on. In this way distributive justice may be more nearly achieved than at present. But greatly increased taxes necessitate extension of government functions. Both local and central agencies will find more to do, and try to solve problems increasingly by appropriating the visible means of production. Equalization of income thus means eventually a restriction of private property as well as a revelation of services. Sumptuary laws may also help in equalizing incomes, but the greatest power for good at all times is education. Socialists therefore insist upon the universalization of enlightenment, and our friends of reform, whether socialistic or otherwise, will support this view. Education is the means of social advancement. More education, and education for more people. Both are needed. Education should be made compulsory and free. It should be open to all regardless of wealth or parentage or aims in life or physical prowess, and it should be in the hands of experts whose services are inferior to none. It is necessary that vocational guidance play a part in the placement of men. It is absolutely essential that technical training be supplemented by instruction in the arts and sciences, natural or social, and there is hardly any doubt but that education up to the twenty-first year should form our minimum of demands, if democracy is to be more than a name.

With this right and duty to learn should be coupled the right and duty to work, after schooling and practicum has duly prepared men for their career. Production at most points is a profession as truly as if it were based on the Liberal Arts. To work well is a duty none can shirk, but the *chance* to work well must form part of the contract. All should be obliged to toil. Idleness is never a gain, but may often turn out to be a vice. Idleness is consumption without production. Leisure is consumption with a view to increased production. Leisure is more than that, but so much at least it means which the life of a wastrel does not mean. There is no excuse for loitering and lolling about in these days of opportunity. The masses should not be expected to work at a treadmill so a few may lead a parasitic existence. Parasites are not necessary in a well-ordered community. But on the other hand, those who have done their share should be allowed to rest in old age. Leisure for rest, for recreation, and for regeneration of productive powers. Leisure for amusement and sport. Leisure for the young, and recuperation for the aged when their strength is on the wane!

These and some other rights to be claimed on behalf of the common folk make up the platform of democracy. Socialists have long adopted it, and friends of progress in all walks of life will call it their own. Democracy should profit by social science, not ignore it in the fatuous belief that because its values are not measurable by physical standards they do not exist. The values of life and of sociation are patent enough to those taking the trouble to study them. They form part of the equipment without which men in charge of public affairs are sure to fail. Socialists have understood them in large measure, but must now agree to further amendments of their original creed, if they wish to enlist the sympathies of thinking people. Revision is wholesome according to their own teachings. Revision is a step in the onward march of civilization. Science itself is nothing if not continual growth and redefinition of terms, whose finest fruit is the advancement of humanism.

It is therefore no disgrace for socialism to have fallen short of its mark, but it would be sad if the lessons it first taught so brilliantly were to be forgotten by reformers to come.

INDEX

PRINTED IN THE UNITED STATES OF AMERICA